Ann Mucke

Melancholy
BABY

Melancholy BABY

The Unplanned Consequences of the G.I.s' Arrival in Europe for World War II

Pamela Winfield

BERGIN & GARVEY
Westport, Connecticut • London

Library of Congress Cataloging-in-Publication Data

Winfield, Pamela.
    Melancholy baby : the unplanned consequences of the G.I.s' arrival in Europe
for World War II / Pamela Winfield.
        p.   cm.
    ISBN 0–89789–639–4 (alk. paper)
    1. World War, 1939–1945—Women—Great Britain.   2. War brides—Great
Britain—History—20th century.   3. Women immigrants—United States—
History—20th century.   I. Title.
    D810.W7W545   2000
    306.2'7—dc21   99–046151

British Library Cataloguing in Publication Data is available.

Library of Congress Catalog Card Number: 99–046151
ISBN: 0–89789–639–4

First published in 2000

Bergin & Garvey, 88 Post Road West, Westport, CT 06881
An imprint of Greenwood Publishing Group, Inc.
www.greenwood.com

Printed in the United States of America

The paper used in this book complies with the
Permanent Paper Standard issued by the National
Information Standards Organization (Z39.48–1984).

10 9 8 7 6 5 4 3 2 1

The author and publisher gratefully acknowledge permission to use the following
photos on the jacket: Photo of Sharyn H. with her father, daughter, and grandchildren
taken by Joan Williams, photographer. Reproduced with permission. Photo of Franklin meeting Pamela in London reproduced by permission of Norma Jean Clarke-
McCloud.

Every reasonable effort has been made to trace the owners of copyright materials in
this book, but in some instances this has proven impossible. The author and publisher will be glad to receive information leading to more complete acknowledgments
in subsequent printings of the book and in the meantime extend their apologies for
any omissions.

This book is in memory of all the G.I.s who passed through the American Red Cross Clubs in the U.K. and, in particular, the Mostyn and Mayflower in London.

Sadly, not all of them made it "Home."

"I thought to lose the ground under my feet and I have had 1000 butterflies in my belly. This feeling is not really to describe and no one can feel and understand the same without it was one in the same situation."

—Dorothea Renoth, Altenmarkt, Germany,
struggling to express her emotion
in a newly learned language.

Contents

Acknowledgments

I would like to thank everyone who agreed to participate in this book by sharing their stories; Sophia Byrne, the invaluable membership secretary of Transatlantic Children's Enterprise; and also Inge Gurr who I had the good fortune to claim as a close neighbor. She not only interpreted the letters from Germany and dealt with the answers but extended my knowledge of German postwar social attitudes.

In addition, a "thank you" is due all the people in Sesser, Illinois, who made me so welcome when I first arrived.

Introduction: "Over-paid, Over-sexed, and Over Here"

It is a sunny spring day in March 1998; I am about to address a ladies' luncheon on what is still the most popular subject on my list of talks: "G.I. Brides and G.I. Babies," which relates to the romances between British women and the G.I.s. The venue is Peterborough, a cathedral city that would have received visits from thousands of G.I.s from 1942 to 1945 because the 8th Air Force was stationed all around the area. As poignant a fact today is that Madingley, the U.S. military cemetery, is not far away, so some of them are still here.

I will know from the smiles, winks, and nudges in my audience that many of the older ladies share happy memories of those hectic wartime years. The magic of Hollywood was suddenly personified by real Americans. Those G.I.s may not all have looked like film stars, but they talked like film stars. Their uniforms were very smart compared to their British counterparts, and they had such charming manners. No one had ever met their like before. Someone in the media, possibly inspired by jealousy, quickly dubbed the American G.I.s "over-paid, over-sexed, and over here." It carries to this day and is not a reputation they deserve. They were normal young men, many from small-town America who had never been far from home until they hit training camp. They came to the United Kingdom to help finish a war that had been dragging on for three years.

The arrival of those G.I.s is a phenomenon that will never happen again, unless men come down from Mars. They left their mark on a large swathe of the British population, especially the young women who were just coming into an adult world, which the war had left alarmingly short of peer-group males.

The impact of these men should never be underestimated. The fact that they were often "first loves" made them even more unforgettable. Dramatic as it may sound to a cynic, some women never got over them; several were heard to murmur his name as they died. The following excerpt from a letter written in 1992 by a mother to her daughter exemplifies the magic many young women felt in meeting a G.I.

> I want you to read this—it may help you understand. It is fifty years this year since I met your *real* father. We were taken to the American base as they hadn't long been here. They gave a dance; the Inkspots were singing "Paper Moon." He had light brown hair and a ready smile. We danced every dance and when it was time to go, we arranged to meet the following Saturday if I could get out of Camp. We went for a drink and a chat and tried to meet as often as we could. Gradually we fell in love. . . . We both shed tears when the order came to go to France. I didn't tell him I was pregnant. I could tell no one, I was so scared. He wrote to me from France and that's when I told him. . . . Did he write letters that got lost or were they kept from me? [She was under a lot of family pressure.] Time went by. . . . Well, it is fifty years now, but I still think of him vividly. I can picture his face so clearly. There has never been a love like I felt for that handsome American for three years. They were the best years of my life—years I would not have missed for anything.

To have a child out of wedlock was unthinkable in prewar Britain. However, it was a common enough outcome of many wartime romances. Another woman writes:

> I had never met an American until I went down to Devon to do some war work as a cook on a farm; assisting with food production was an important part of the war effort. The only place in the village nearby to socialize was the pub. We heard some rumours that G.I.s would be arriving. Then one evening, a crowd of them burst in. The pub was heated with a coal fire; the custom was that whoever was the closest topped it up as necessary. As I began to do this, a voice said "Allow me." I went to jelly, it was love at first sight. Within a few weeks, we were seriously making love, first in the fields, then we went to an

hotel. There was an urgency in the air; we all knew that the Invasion of France was imminent. The bombing was dreadful. When I discovered that I was pregnant, he was shocked when I said, "you'll go back and you'll forget me." But, he didn't. Once the Invasion succeeded and they were "dug in," he sent letters and money. I told my sister first and asked her not to tell our mother but I had a difficult time with the pregnancy and she insisted. Mum was marvelous and now she knew, I felt better. I stayed with my sister until the war ended, then came back to London. Christine was four months old. Letters, presents, and care packages arrived from Jack. I used my savings to enable me to stay home with the baby for a year. Then I put her in a day nursery and went to work for Marks and Spencers. After eight years, I gave up on Jack sending for us and got on with my life. I found out later that he was terrified to tell his mother that he had left us behind. Christine eventually found him with the help of TRACE. I have no regrets, I have a marvelous daughter and two grandsons.

TRACE—the Transatlantic Children's Enterprise—is the organization I helped found in 1986 after I wrote the book *Sentimental Journey* and BBC 2 did a documentary on G.I. brides with a segment on the children left behind. In response to that show, many letters were sent to the studio by people who were children of G.I.s wanting to find their fathers. I have been helping people make contact ever since.

At this lunch in 1998, I am accompanied by the offspring of a wartime liaison. I am a G.I. bride, and she is a G.I. baby. We can both be counted in tens of thousands. Today I will shorten my talk so that she can give an account of the emotion attached to her circumstances.

As will be revealed, the children of the G.I.s in Europe are as big a cross-section of lifestyles as their fathers were, pre- or postwar. They are involved in all aspects of European life; one in Germany was a leading member of the Green Party. The daughter of one of the G.I.s who chose to return to live in the U.K. was co-designer of the Princess of Wales's wedding dress, is a prominent name in the fashion world, and was present at Diana's funeral.

Chapter One

The U.S. Navy Afloat in London

"America" was a magic word to me from childhood. We were a generation that went to the movies at least once a week. In 1939, I remember wishing hard that I could go to the World's Fair in New York. By then, I had an extra incentive. I had met an American member of the family—an impressive man in a navy chalk-striped suit who owned a cinema! His father, the eldest brother on my paternal side, had emigrated to the United States after World War I and settled in Philadelphia.

When World War II broke out, some children were evacuated to America. I begged to be allowed to go, but my father felt that regardless of the potential danger of bombing (school and homelife were punctuated with air raids), we should stay together. His refusal was justified when one of the ships full of children was torpedoed in the Atlantic.

Then came Pearl Harbor, and the United States entered the war. Troops were on their way to the U.K.—real Americans just like we had seen in the movies. I wondered if I would have the chance to meet any of them. At the time, this appeared unlikely. I was in a single-sex school, and any contact with males was forbidden by a very strict father. However, in my senior year, I was allowed a little more social freedom, which I managed to extend to include the Saturday night dance at our local town hall. To me that was the height of sophistication before the war. I had seen ladies sweeping

Melancholy Baby

in wearing evening dress. Off I went with a warning to be home by 10:30 P.M.

At first the dance did not appear to be much fun. The war had caused a shortage of males on the home front; women were dancing with women. Suddenly, the air was electrified by the arrival of a crowd of G.I.s. They came from a base two stops down the line. We British girls shared a collective response—"Wow!"

Compared to the girls they had left behind, so fashionably adorned as illustrated in the movies, we must have looked a drab lot given the limitations of clothes rationing. However, a smiling female is a great attraction to a lonely soldier.

We made friends fast on the dance floor, but I did not dare go into the bar at the back where the G.I.s were buying drinks for everyone during the interval. I did not have the courage to pretend that I was old enough to be admitted. One amused G.I., seeing my look of longing, offered a roll of Lifesavers. This was my first experience of candy with a hole in it.

From then on, my first dance was a great success. Before the evening was over, I had wheedled a USAF button off one of the men as a souvenir. I wore it on my school uniform the following Monday. My friends were horrified; nice girls were not supposed to go out with Yanks, who had already acquired something of a racy reputation. They were known to whistle at girls walking down the street, even pick them up on trains or at bus stops. Man shortage or not at that time, in my circle this was disapproved. Girls like me were supposed to be formally introduced or have some bona fide reason to accept a social invitation from an unknown person.

Since I thought these G.I.s were great fun, I had to find a way around my dilemma. This came when I heard that one could volunteer for the American Red Cross. Many clubs were being established around the country near the bases and in London for the G.I.s coming on leave (let alone the large number stationed close by). This not only solved my social problem but made me feel useful. I was too young to go into uniform yet, but at least I could now contribute to the war effort.

Accompanied by an agreeable school friend as excited as I was at the prospect of meeting some of these G.I.s, I applied to the head office of the American Red Cross, which was situated in Grosvenor Square in London, near the American Embassy. As we walked in, the mere sound of those American voices was exhilarating. Only one problem arose when we filled in the application forms; we were not yet 18 and needed parental permission. Once we had it, we were cleared for takeoff.

With our backgrounds I had expected that we would be sent to one of the Officers' Clubs, but given our age, which would make us "jail bait" (until then an unknown expression to me), we were assigned to an Enlisted Men's Club where the majority of the young servicemen were teenagers too. We arrived with so little knowledge of the difference in language that when I went into the ladies' room and read a sign that said "prophylactics are available at the Main Desk," I assumed this was yet another new kind of candy. Fortunately, I never made the mistake of asking for some.

Our Red Cross Club was in Portman Square, London, and had been a hotel before the war. On arrival, we were sent down to the canteen in the basement and handed voluminous white overalls bearing the insignia of the American Red Cross. We had been on food rationing for three years by then, so the sight of all the food on display was overwhelming. We were given the choice of clearing tables after the men had eaten (which would give us a chance to chat) or dispensing soup from a large, hissing urn. Quick to see the advantage of mixing with the men, we volunteered to be waitresses.

We soon learned that these G.I.s were mostly small-town boys, many fresh out of high school. Few had been far from home until they enlisted; all were bug-eyed at being in London. They were a delight with their fascinating accents and quick to wisecrack about my lack of expertise as a waitress. I came from a home with domestic help and had absolutely no idea how to pile a tray with dirty dishes, let alone first balance it securely on the table. My breakage level was very high.

From where we worked, we could hear music that came from the nightly dances. We were warned that we could not attend unless invited. This began to happen quite frequently, but we felt a little like Cinderellas as we emerged from those bulky overalls. This feeling was heightened when we began to notice women arriving already dressed to dance in the limited finery that wartime allowed. We also discovered that there was a more preferable job to be had in the American Red Cross—a dance hostess!

We applied to change jobs and, once it was agreed, made preparations for our new role. Clothes rationing precluded buying anything frivolous. I did have the advantage of a father in the clothing business, but all I got out of that was a long piece of cloth. It was up to me to transform it into the pleated skirt I desired. Without access to or knowledge of how to operate a sewing machine, this was done by hand. Meanwhile, my friend Marie unpicked two old skirts, and reformed them into something similar. Then we practiced in front of the mirror, twirling around to achieve the quick flash of panties that we had seen in the movies. We were ready to be dance hostesses.

Our new assignment was a much larger Red Cross Club, and to my astonishment it was full of sailors who were attached to the 6th Fleet Headquarters in North Audley Street, London. I had never had occasion to meet a sailor before; they were not a feature of the suburban town where I lived.

Jitterbugging across the floor came a red-headed sailor who without missing a beat drew me onto the dance floor. We very quickly became an "item," and I learned that he was from a small town in Illinois and was making the Navy his career. I never matched him as a dancer, but we both agreed that we would like to share a future. Thus, I became one of what the British press christened "G.I. brides." I was in good company. Though figures vary, there were to be at least 60,000 of us, numbers that took the U.S. authorities completely by surprise.

In hindsight, the explanation for these large numbers may be quite simple. Without access to the spacious backseat of an American car, courting rituals in England were severely limited. Also, the mores of the day meant that a girl was supposed to wear a wedding ring before she took a man to her bed. That is not to say that many did not take chances, but there was a great reluctance on the part of men at that time to use the prophylactics that were freely available on base. Many chose to take their chances, accepting the code of that time that if the girl did get pregnant, one did the right thing and married her!

Either method worked well until the imminent invasion of France emptied all the bases in the U.K. and left the brides and the pregnant sweethearts waiting for their G.I.s to come back for them when the war was over. Only in a few cases were they able to.

The return of the G.I. to the United States would not follow the same pattern as his arrival in Europe. Troopships took them directly from France to the United States, sailing up the English Channel without stopping. On one or two of the ships that did stop for supplies at Southampton, a few men jumped ship with the inevitable consequences of military punishment, which could be as severe as a dishonorable discharge. The majority of the men could not voice their disappointment at not being able to collect their British brides until they arrived home. There, they had strict immigration laws to contend with. Delay was inevitable.

The G.I. brides were transformed into G.I. wallflowers by the British press as they waited to be sent for. At that time entry by immigrants into the United States was restricted to low numbers. A change in the law would be required before these British wives and children would be allowed in. Some of the more militant of the women heard that Mrs. Eleanor Roosevelt, the widow of the late president, had arrived in London for a conference and was staying at Claridges. They marched up and down in front of her hotel with banners and babies demanding help to join their husbands.

One can only conjecture on how much this helped facilitate the bill approved by the White House in December 1945. Through it, the brides became a moment in history. It waived the existing law to allow the alien spouses of servicemen who had served honorably in the armed forces in World War II and their children to be allowed in. We became the largest group of immigrants allowed in since the turn of the century and the forerunners of all the other nationalities of war brides that would follow. Their numbers eventually exceeded two million.

The implementation of the new law became the responsibility of the U.S. Army Transport Division. They reassembled some of the ships that had originally brought the G.I.s to Europe. The fleet was a combination of liners like the *Queen Mary*, the USS *Argentinia*, and SS *Washington* and ships which fitted better into the category of "rust buckets."

Once this was organized, travel orders went out to the brides. The paperwork included labels, similar in style to those attached to school children who were evacuated in wartime. Beside the passenger's name was stamped "Head Tax paid," a charge that was obligatory for immigrants at that time. This, like the cost of the voyage, was paid by the U.S. Government.

Our instructions included a date of departure. The official start of our journey to our husbands would be from Waterloo, a mainline London railway station still scarred from wartime bombing. It became a scene of chaos as women, the majority of us with babes in arms, arrived from all over the U.K. They were often accompanied by tearful parents who recognized the finality of the farewell. One has to remember that it was still a time when, from the U.K., the United States seemed as distant as another planet. Add to this the fact that travel was beyond most peoples' means. They doubted that they would ever see their daughters and grandchildren again.

This led to emotional, lingering farewells as the brides recognized the reality of their actions. The porters on hand to assist in the boarding of the train eventually had to physically push some of the passengers into the carriages. Their initial destinations had links with the G.I.s they had married, such as the barracks on Salisbury Plain, used by some prior to the invasion of France and Bournemouth, or the Carlton, a luxury hotel that had been commandeered in wartime as a rest and relaxation center for the United States Air Force and would now be used to process some of their brides prior to their journey to the States.

We were decanted at the station into buses for the last lap of the journey. There were by now some very fractious passengers including tearful women already homesick. Few had been very far from home before. Many who had not had the full responsibility of their children before were already worn out with the struggle of the journey so far and fearful that they could not manage without their mothers. Several refused to leave the buses when they arrived and insisted on returning home.

The majority of us refused to be daunted. We were shepherded through to the reception area. Here the first request was proof that we had had a smallpox vaccination, as advised on our travel papers. This was an obligatory requirement at that time for anyone entering the United States. Those who had ignored this injunction were taken to the medical officer to have it done.

We were informed that we would be assigned three to a room, which would be no hardship since before the war the Carlton had been a four-star hotel. I went upstairs to find my room, and it was already occupied by a very homesick Cockney girl who was turning the air blue with obscenities. While I did not know such swear words existed, I must confess to learning them very fast.

More fascinating to me, though, was the fact that she was wearing an American dress. Up until then, I had only seen them in the movies. Hers had a zipper that went all the way down the back. This to me was a most elegant luxury since we were a buttons-and-bows generation. To have even a short zipper on a skirt was the height of sophistication.

I quickly learned that that dress constituted her whole travel wardrobe. The rest of her luggage was equally limited: two diapers tucked round the baby in its carrycot and one feeding bottle. She was from a very poor family and had left everything else for her Mum to supplement the clothes rationing that was still in force. Since it cost one clothing coupon for a towel or diaper (British ones at that time were made of towelling), they could serve the same use.

Into the room then came the third person who would make up our trio. She was carrying a red-headed baby. The inevitable questions we asked as we all met each other was, "Where are you going?" I had already discovered that the Cockney girl was going to Boston, so I now turned to this newcomer with a baby that had hair that matched my baby's and asked again. I was somewhat stunned by her reply. She was going to Illinois, and so was I! We stared at each other's babies and, quite forgetting the paperwork that had preceded our arrival at this hotel, thought that we might have married the same man. Our wedding photographs quickly confirmed that we had not.

With Illinois in common, we were instantly bonded. When we later examined the selection of Americana on view in the main hall, we discovered our destinations were only nineteen miles apart. This made us all the more determined to try to travel together. It proved simple once we recognized the procedure. At dinner each evening, the organizer would inform a group of tables that they were the next to go. If we stayed together for meals we had a good chance.

I am told that some girls went to bed at night praying that they would get on the *Queen Mary*. Eunice and I were not to be that fortunate. When we were bused down to the port in Southampton, an elderly relic of troop-carrying duties, the *Edmund B. Alexander*, was waiting.

Our delight at having the same cabin number was somewhat diluted by the discovery that it contained bunks stacked three high to accommodate thirty-two women. This left little space to unpack. Suitcases were piled high in corners and clothes draped around any available knob. Our babies did better, they had a nursery that was staffed by army nurses. They were wonderful to the children but not very impressed with us.

We were still better off than some of the brides on other sailings. Space was so limited that they had to keep their babies with them in the bunks. This caused some appalling accidents. Fortunately, those with toddler-age children had the security of small cabins. There were also brides who faltered at the gangplank. One must remember that before the war few of them had been any farther from home than the nearest town. At the sight of the sea, they lost their spirit of adventure. They, like the earlier women who had refused to get off the bus when it reached the hotel, now went home. In some cases, the G.I. husbands were able to come over to the U.K. and persuade them to give the United States a try. Others were simply divorced.

As the G.I. bride ships sailed out of Southampton, they sometimes passed shiploads of British servicemen who were still returning from the war overseas. The men would lean over the side yelling, "You'll be sorry!" The girls would shout back, "No, we won't!" What some of those men were yet to discover was that they were returning to a Yankee "cuckoo" in their nest.

I was actually sailing away from my husband, who was by now stationed in occupied Germany, but he planned to take leave and meet me in New York so that he could accompany me to southern Illinois and introduce me to his family. We were then to return to Germany together.

The canteen on our ship was reminiscent of the first Red Cross club I had worked in and still in the equivalent position, the lowest deck. It was the same canteen style. I already had some experience of how different American food was, but a lot of the other brides did not take kindly to any of it, especially pineapple on their ham or creamed corn.

Once out in the heavy swell of the Atlantic, seasickness became inevitable. My original solution was to dash down to the mess, grab a roll and butter, and bring it up on deck to eat. Then, one of the crew advised sucking a lemon. This worked, and from then on I never went anywhere without one in my hand.

Within a couple of days at sea, an announcement came over the Tannoy that we were all to have a medical examination. We were ordered to be in our bunks, unclothed and wait for the doctor to come round. Some of the women had hysterics; modesty was the order of their era. The more sensible of us finally convinced them that there was little danger to their reputation with so many of us present. The young doctor who arrived was obviously more terrified of us than we of him. Protected by a burly sailor with a clip board, he sidled from bunk to bunk for a quick removal of sheets and a brief flashlight inspection. I suspect that he dined out on that episode for years.

Our ship was very much a social, cultural, and geographic mix, which induced criticisms of background aimed more at the highest than lowest level. The only thing that we had in common was the fact that we had all married G.I.s. This had yet to imbue us with American-style equality. In such crowded conditions there were bound to be squabbles over territorial rights that could literally involve square inches of deck.

In an effort to keep us busy and out of trouble, the ship's crew arranged various activites. Lectures on life in America were well attended but misleadingly framed with white, picket-fenced houses, a far cry from what so many of these women were to find.

Volunteers were requested to perform in a show on the last night of the voyage. Eunice and I offered ourselves for the chorus. As Eunice had sung in her church choir back in her hometown of Luton, she was also asked to do a solo. Somewhat appropriately, she chose "Wanting You," a popular concert number of that period. The song selected for the finale was "They'll Always Be an England." The cast and audience dissolved into tears. It brought home to them the fact that they would probably never see it again. One has to remember that these were not the usual kind of immigrants. It was love for their G.I. husband, not necessarily need for a new life, that was bringing them across the Atlantic.

At dawn of the day we arrived, most of us were already crowding the deck dressed in our best suits, gloves, and Deanna Durbin hats.

Not everyone yet had the luxury of nylon stockings and were consequently bare-legged, a fact not lost on the reporters who came out in a launch for first interviews. One of them posed the stocking-less girls in a hem-raised, crooked-knee line to demonstrate how much they were looking forward to unrationed hose.

As we entered the New York harbor, the magic of America began to unfold just like Hollywood had promised. There was the Statue of Liberty, skyscrapers, and great big flashy American cars going along the coastal road. As we came closer a waiting military band began to play "Sentimental Journey." Down on the quay were husbands waving like mad. Not all the wives waved back because their men were out of uniform and did not look the same; Fedora hats, zoot suits, and leather jackets made them unrecognizable. In a state of shock, some ran back to their cabins, locked themselves in, and refused to emerge until the ship turned back for England.

Those with husbands meeting them had been instructed to attach their labels to their jackets and wait in the vicinity of the purser's office to be collected. I knew by now that my husband would not be among them; halfway across the Atlantic I had received word that he was delayed in Germany. I would now be meeting my in-laws on my own. Although they had sent me welcoming letters, this was still a daunting prospect.

Eunice already knew that she would not see her husband until she reached Illinois. He, like many other G.I.s at that time, could not afford the fare to New York to pick up his wife. It was the first of the surprises that were ahead. Those G.I.s in the U.K. who had seemed to have so much money did not necessarily have the same kind of funds as civilians in the States.

Eunice and I received what were to me confusing train tickets. My husband had said we would go from New York to Chicago and thence south to his hometown. What we were given indicated that we were going down the east coast of America before turning inland. Since I had never travelled any farther than ninety miles north of London at that time, I was in no position to argue. In any case, as Eunice and I were together, I saw no need to worry. In retrospect, I can see where the Army Transport Division sought to get us all as close as possible to our destinations. We girls had no comprehension at that time of the enormous size of the United States. Some were overwhelmed when they discovered that they had another 3,000 miles to go before they would be united with their husbands.

A fleet of army cars arrived to take us on to our various stations. Eunice and I were driven through New York where we were astonished at the shop windows stuffed with goods, which, due to wartime shortages, we had forgotten existed. We had truly left clothes rationing and food rationing behind forever. Our driver obviously took note of our excited comments. When we arrived at our station with half an hour to spare, he offered to watch the sleeping babies if we wanted to do a little shopping. We took off at a run, and our first purchases were dainty shoes, which had been in such short supply in wartime England. Mine were navy, platform-soled, and decorated with brass studs. Eunice bought the same style in white. We were elated to finally have something American to wear.

Next came our first taste of American luxury: We were assigned seats in a Pullman coach. The porter appeared very quickly to see what he could do to help. Our first request proved a problem when we asked him to warm our baby bottles. Ours were boat-shaped and he had never seen anything like that before. However, with a little applied Yankee ingenuity, he managed.

Our train stopped in Washington, D.C., and it was held up so that Eunice and I could run down the platform for a glimpse of the skyline of what was now to be our Capitol. Questions as to the reasons for the delay then alerted the rest of the passengers to the fact there were war brides on board. People began to drift along the corridors to have a look at us. Some stopped to chat; one lady was quick to assure me that she knew how bad the wartime air raids had been because she had heard them on the radio. My joking answer that she had been fortunate to hear rather than suffer one brought a blank stare. This was a swift reminder that in spite of our appreciation of Bob Hope and Jack Benny beamed out on the American Forces Radio Network, there were still some differences to overcome with some kind of humor.

However, we all shared a laugh when one man asked us where we came from. We explained that we had just gotten off the boat. He expressed astonishment that we spoke such good English. Most people just wanted to hear our British accents, and since we were to be two days and nights on the train there was ample opportunity. What came to us as a great surprise in our conversations was the fact that not everyone in the United States revered Roosevelt as we had in England. In meeting these Republicans, we had our first taste of American politics.

With two babies and no disposable diapers invented yet, laundry began to be a problem. The war had taught us to be adaptable, so we took the string off our shoe boxes to make a little line in the ladies' room and were very thankful that in spite of the plush surroundings no one complained about our drying baby clothes.

Eunice was due to be the first one to get off the train, but when we arrived at her stop, all we saw was a small depot burned to the ground, and there was no one there to meet her. Before we left England we had read several horror stories in the press about brides being deserted once they reached their destination. Was this to be Eunice's fate? Rather than take the chance, I suggested that she should stay on the train with me.

Research would later show that mistakes were made in the rush of official arrangements, rather than the blame resting on husbands. One can only imagine the terror suffered by these young women let off trains in obscure, tiny towns, often up in the mountains, in the early hours of the morning. A few did disappear without trace.

At my stop there was a reception committee waiting; my mother-in-law and her youngest son and daughter. They were not expecting two women to get off the train, and the fact we were each carrying a red-headed baby added to the confusion. My mother-in-law, a staunch, natural born American, unswervingly believed, as many did at that time, that hers was the greatest country in the world. (Some could not understand why their sons had not waited to marry "healthy" American women.) She would later tell me that her first thought on seeing us was that because we came from a "foreign" country, her son had been allowed to marry two women.

Once we explained the situation, Eunice phoned her husband and discovered that he was one of the men who had not been notified of the date or place of his wife's arrival. When he heard that my destination was Sesser, Illinois, he told her that it would be closer than if she waited at the station in Odin. We all squeezed into the car to set off for my husband's hometown.

I had not been told any exaggerated stories about my husband's background. I already knew that his father was a coal miner and that his parents lived in a house made of wood. That sounded rather quaint and rustic as did the fact it was not plumbed. Since I was not expecting to stay there long before embarking for Germany, it sounded like an American adventure.

I had always been an avid reader of all things American, and to acquaint myself with this phase of my new life I had read *How Green Was My Valley* because I thought that there would be some similarity between British and American coal miners. I soon discovered that between the two nationalities was a great divide. Added to that, my in-laws' house looked smaller than any I had seen in the movies. It was painted white, but it did not have a picket fence.

My father-in-law was waiting at the side, wearing bib overalls. They were not to be a fashion item for many years, so I had never seen them close up before. Certainly, no one that I knew in England wore them. He turned out to be a delightful, log-cabin-born American who would fascinate me with stories of his primitive, country childhood.

He was very proud of his modest house, but in my honor they had laid on running water in the kitchen. There was no bathroom. The outside toilet was the greater surprise because this was something that I thought I knew about. We had outside toilets in our London suburb. They were always plumbed and convenient to the back door—useful if one had been out in the garden. The one in Sesser looked quite impressive; it had imitation brick siding and was located at the end of a concrete path. But, between it and me stepping off the back porch was a flock of chickens commanded by a rooster. That was the most anti-British bird I ever met. I always had to have an escort to the outhouse.

My father-in-law did not go to work on a bicycle like the British coal miners. He was picked up in a big, flashy American car and came home as clean as he departed. Before he left at 5:00 A.M. he shook down the ashes of the stove in the living room, which heated the house. There was never any need for an alarm clock. We were all awake from then on.

I was in what is now called "culture shock." Sesser, Illinois, had a population of 2,100. Main Street was three blocks away from the family house and consisted of four bars, a corner grocery (no supermarkets yet), a dry goods store, a dime store, and a drug store, in which was a soda fountain with high stools. This was the town's only comparison with any movie I had seen. There, I became an addict of pineapple marshmallow ice cream sundaes until my alarming increase in weight brought this to a halt.

My English pram was part of the "hold" luggage on the ship and did not arrive until a couple of weeks later. It was a source of wonder to everyone in the town who had never seen such a "contraption" before. Pushing the baby in it was not simple without sidewalks. Everything was proving different, including the birds. In the U.K. the G.I.s had scoffed at the tiny robins and said in America that they were much larger. They said that about so many things, and none of us believed it until we saw the size of the American robins. (They are not the same species and belong to the thrush family.) Another surprise were the blackbirds. I trailed one round the garden—sorry, yard—concerned that it was bleeding. Amid family laughter I was told that it belonged to the redwing variety.

Certain things that they took for granted were totally new experiences for me. I had come from a home with a live-in maid; the laundry was collected and delivered weekly. Here, my mother-in-law, as yet to have a washing machine, had a weekly laundry ritual.

Out came the scrubbing board, water heated on the stove, rinse and bleach tubs prepared in a row. Anxious to pull my weight, I volunteered to help and suggested that I hang out the washing. With absolutely no idea of how to do this, I left a line of clothes that looked like they were doing acrobatics. I was not asked to do this again.

As an only child, I found being part of this large family exhilarating. All the married siblings lived in the town, and we gathered together for Sunday lunch. I was introduced to fried chicken, which I loved once I had overcome the picture of my mother-in-law, hatchet in hand, decapitating the birds in the morning. Cherry pie with whipped cream topping stands out as the first of my favorite American deserts.

What did take me a while to get used to was that instead of a mix of sexes round the table, the women served the men first. Then, I discovered that this was part of American history and dated back to when the men came in from laboring in the fields and were therefore entitled to first choice of the food. I soon learned that an all-female table could be great fun, even though it was then up to us to clear away and wash all the dishes.

Some of the phrases that I was hearing were also historic. At first, I did not understand my mother-in-law when she offered me a cup of "tay" or if she told me to "pay it no mind." I later learned that they were a vestige of Shakespearean English, which had been retained by these small American communities cut off from the mainstream.

Eunice and I were able to share these early experiences of adjustment. She was living in similar, small-town circumstances in a house owned by her in-laws. While it was unplumbed, she did have the luxury of a pump attached to her kitchen sink, which saved having to haul water from the well. Her husband, Don, had returned to college under the G.I. Bill. While I waited for my husband to come on leave from Germany and collect me, Eunice and I saw each other frequently. We alleviated our homesickness with cups of real leaf tea. Fortunately, that was as common then to find as tea bags, which took some getting used to, as did wire coat hangers that had a tendency to tangle.

When I later discussed this period of adjustment with other war brides, certain amusing and sometimes embarassing incidents were revealed. What stood out most was the unexpectedness of Grace before meals, rarely practiced in the U.K. Other more sad incidents were revealed. One war bride constantly criticized "We don't do that in England," which seemed like a threat to her daughter; she thought that mother would return there. She is now a confirmed Anglophobe. My son assumed that all mothers spoke with English accents and fathers American until he went to school. The other language barrier was when these British women who had rarely heard a foreign accent prior to the war, found themselves living in Polish- or Italian-speaking areas, which were more prevalent then. Not all of them were well received and struggled in alien surroundings. A few found that while their children were welcome, they were not. This made some cut and run for fear of losing them. The majority overcame their homesickness, enjoyed their lives, and produced a generation of children who have added to the American culture.

Eunice, like me and most of the rest, became an American citizen. Her husband was called back into the Reserve when the Korean War broke out. After that, Don decided to make the Air Force his career. So Eunice also became a service wife and travelled extensively. She now lives in Virginia and is very active in the Transatlantic Brides and Parents' Association (TBPA). The norm was that if two war brides got together it was to share a cup of tea and reminisce—three and there was the nucleus for a club. Clubs began to form all over the United States. The one in Vienna, Virginia, is so long established that they are like a family. Eunice and I stay in contact with each other to this day.

Chapter Two

۶ᵔ๑ᵔ๑ᵕ

"Service Wife"

When my husband arrived in Sesser a few weeks later, it was with
the grim news that occupied Germany was still not considered fit
for dependents. I would have to stay on in the States longer than we
had anticipated. This news clouded our precious time together,
which, of course, I had to share with his family. When we went to
see him off at the station, I could not bear to wave goodbye.

Without any preparation or luggage, but sure that my mother-in-
law would take care of the baby, I jumped on the train. At least we
could enjoy the journey to Chicago and have an extra day together
before he travelled on to New York to board a ship for Germany. As
a Londoner, I assumed that it would be a simple matter to cash a
check in Chicago for some spending money. I was in for a nasty
shock. There was no branch banking in the United States nor would
the Bank of Chicago honor a check from the bank in Sesser without
first confirming that we had the funds. Credit cards were still a rare
luxury and beyond the expectation of a Navy man, even if he had
been promoted to chief petty officer. This was also prior to fax ma-
chines, so we had to make a long distance telephone call for a trifling
sum of about $20, which was low on the list of telephone priorities.
Our day in Chicago was spent on a stone bench in a marble hall
while we waited to be declared solvent. By the time the money arrived, all it could be used for was a taxi so that I could accompany
my husband to the train for New York.

While I waited in Sesser, the family did their best to keep me busy, happy, and occupied. There were fishing trips and cookouts at the river and visits to extended family members who owned farms. This increased my knowledge of the American language. I learned that wheat, not corn, was grown for flour. Corn, which I knew as "maize," grew on a cob. Also, "pepper" could be a vegetable—green or red—not only something one shook out of a shaker.

I did not realize how much detail of this small-town life would stay in my subconscious for future use. All I saw and knew at that time was how fascinating it all was. For example, mail was not necessarily delivered to the door, and the postmaster knew everyone in town. My youngest brother-in-law was still in high school, so we compared notes on what made his different from mine. Graduation balls and high school yearbooks seemed a much more impressive end to school days than I had had.

As time went by and it began to appear that I would be in Sesser longer than on a temporary basis, I decided that I needed my own space. There had not yet been a recovery in house building, so facilities to rent were limited. I settled for a rooming house over a cavernous bar, which was empty except for a couple of tables and a juke box. I had two rooms with shared bathroom facilities and became part of a hive of families reassembling now that their fathers were back from the war. Among them was one of my sisters-in-law, with whom I had already established a close friendship. The long, dark, musty hall became our social center and while there were occasional bouts of drunken behavior among the tenants, there was very little squabbling and a lot of jollity.

It would be a year before my orders arrived to join my husband in Germany. I would learn later that in his impatience for us to start a family life he had endangered his career by jumping ranks to put the case before the captain. Once I had a date of departure it was simpler to close up the little apartment and move back in with my in-laws for the final few weeks. Anxious as I now was to join my husband, when it came time to say goodbye to my new family I found it hard.

I planned two stops on the journey to New York; the first in Delaware where my school friend who had worked with me in the American Red Cross was now living with her sailor husband. Marie was adjusting to life in Wilmington, which, while much larger a town than Sesser, was suffering a similar housing shortage. She was having to share a home with her in-laws. In most cases this required, but did not always receive, toleration on both sides. Marie was making the best she could of her situation. As much as we both agreed we were enjoying our new world, it was wonderful to be together again with someone we each had known from before we came to America. We drank a lot of tea and compared notes on all the shopping that we had done, then debated the adoption of long skirts now coming into fashion. Our farewells were tearful.

My second stop was to be Philadelphia to meet the rest of the American branch of my father's family. As the train approached, the similarity of the skyline to London's made me extremely homesick. I was finally in a large city again; the sight of busy streets and the smell of dirt was wonderful. My cousins, stylishly decked out in the new, long Dior skirts, were waiting. It was strange to hear American accents coming from people with our family name. They made me so welcome that, by the time I left, it was another tearful farewell.

My debarkation was to be processed at Fort Hamilton, New Jersey. When I arrived, the snow was knee deep—something I had never seen before. Never mind those new long skirts, my first purchase had to be a pair of tall boots. My friend Marie had already briefed me on the ship I would be sailing on because it was the same one that had brought her over to the States. The *Thomas H. Barry* was much more modern than the one I had come over on. I shared a cabin with another mother, and we had cots for the children. Since my son was walking by now, I was also glad of the supervised play area. In addition, the ship had an elegant dining room.

The only problem was that February was not a month to be recommended for sailing across the Atlantic. It was very rough, and rims had to be kept up around the tables to prevent meals from sliding into our laps. Once again, I had procured a lemon and was able to keep seasickness at bay. Harder to deal with were the twinkling lights of England as the voyage neared its end and we sailed up the Channel. I wished that we could have made an extra stop.

My husband was on the dock to meet me in Bremerhaven, Germany. The country had been divided into American, British, French, and Russian zones, but Bremerhaven was declared an international port. It was a bomb-shattered relic of its past glory. I could see the reason for the delay in allowing dependents in to join their husbands. I wondered what sort of accommodation was ahead for us, inland in Bremen. At least the war had given me some experience in adapting to life in air-raid-damaged housing.

I was to have a pleasant surprise. The Allies had commandeered properties that were in reasonable shape. Our new home was a four-bedroom villa in a suburban enclave that seemed untouched by the war. Each dependent family house came complete with a maid who was custodian of the property. Given the conditions in Germany at that time, it was a prestigious job. She had warmth in winter, the security of a salary, a meal while on duty, and leftover food to take home. Previous social standing had no bearing on the present. In such adverse conditions as they now suffered, it was not unusual for a high-ranking German officer's wife (or widow) to be willing to scrub floors for an American sailor's lady.

There was virtually no local economy. Germans scrabbled for what they could find. We dependents were bused fifteen miles to the U.S. Army Commissary for our groceries. The German people, still in shock at their defeat and close to starving, were often seen scavenging around the garbage cans of Allied families. (Even potato peelings could be turned into a nourishing soup.)

My husband had surprised me at the port by being in possession of a car. He had bought it for several cartons of cigarettes on the thriving black market. Anything and everything from cars (the Germans did not have access to or money for gasoline) to diamonds, artwork, and porcelain was traded off for cigarettes, coffee, lard, and other foodstuffs. Eventually the black market would be recognized by the authorities to the extent that space would be allowed in some towns to assist in these exchanges, which could give a little quality to the locals' lives.

There was at first a prohibition against friendly relations between conqueror and conquered. This was supposed to shield Allied soldiers from leftover Nazi propaganda and from any die-hard resistance forces. By 1947, when I arrived, the law against fraternization had disintegrated, almost by popular demand. Many of my husband's friends had German girls on their arms at parties. These girls knew that they risked parental disapproval for "sleeping with the enemy," but they were hungry for male company, let alone the benefits of an American boyfriend.

My greater concern was to make up for the long interval since I had married and could establish a home and a family life for my husband and my son. Our house was quite large, so I was willing to supplement the work of the maid with a housekeeper. We heard of a woman who had been a pharmacist before the war who was looking for a job because there was no longer any demand in Germany for her skills. Her husband was a prisoner of war in a Russian camp and unlikely to be released for a long time. That was how Hela came into our lives. She became as much a friend as an employee and delighted in acting as nanny for my son. They formed a mutual admiration society, and through her I improved my German vocabulary, which I only briefly encountered in college. Every new phrase I heard her use added to my conversational abilities in the local language.

German civilians were prohibited the use of guns of any kind, and wildlife was ravaging the few crops that they were beginning to establish. It was therefore requested that American forces try to solve this problem. My husband was delighted with the opportunity to go hunting. On his first expedition, he returned with a couple of wild hares, which were the size of small ponies. Having skinned and dismembered them, he suggested that I had the basis for our first dinner party.

My knowledge of cooking was almost nil other than domestic science classes at school, and they were limited by the shortage of food in Britain during the war. Nor, while I was in the States, had I ever needed to do more than a minimal amount of cooking for myself and my small son in our apartment. All I had for reference were my observations of my mother-in-law's kitchen back in Illinois.

My husband said all I had to do was fry these pieces of hare, so I attempted to replicate memories of delicious Sesser-style chicken. My first dinner party had to be written off as a disaster. All I achieved was barely cooked, tough pieces of hare. I learned later that I should have par-boiled them first!

In spite of that setback, I was beginning to feel settled. I soon learned that this is a dangerous state of mind for a service wife. After a few months, my husband came home with orders for Frankfurt. Unlike the international status of Bremen, this town was in the official American zone. While service personnel could cross borders, German nationals were forbidden to stray from home territories—in this case, to go beyond the British zone boundaries. Regardless, there was no question of leaving Hela behind, she was now not only part of the family but would have been homeless. There was as yet no sign of her husband being returned from Russia. I made an official request on her behalf. It was turned down. Undeterred, I looked for a way to smuggle her out. This came in the shape of the U.S. Navy truck sent to help move our belongings. With the compliance of the two-sailor crew, it became a perfect hiding place for Hela. Leading off with our car, we made for Hanover and then crossed a bridge over the deep and wide River Weser, which brought to life a favorite poem, "The Pied Piper of Hamlin," but without the rats!

Driving in a southeasterly direction, we were soon safely in the American zone going over autobahns that had been left mostly unscarred to facilitate the movement of advancing Allied troops. I was fascinated by signposts pointing off to towns that I had heard mentioned as sites for British and American wartime bombing raids.

Frankfurt had received its share of damage. The downtown area was barely walkable. There was a heavy, odd, and unpleasant smell in the air, which turned out to be bodies, unremoved from the enormous amount of ruined buildings because the town's infrastructure had yet to be restored. The only building completely undamaged was on the outskirts, owned by I. G. Farben. It had been deliberately left intact to provide offices for the occupying forces.

The dependent housing did not turn out to be as grand as what I had enjoyed in Bremen. The authorities had taken over an area of modest, three-bedroom, terraced houses in a suburb called Heddernheim and surrounded them with barbed wire. Each house had a maid who came in on a daily basis. The entry gates to the compound were guarded by Polish former German prisoners of war, who harbored bitter memories of their treatment. Their position presented them with the opportunity to get back at the Germans.

The local food situation was no better in Frankfurt than in Bremen, therefore the maids were appreciative of any leftovers, which in an American household were bountiful. What were treasured the most were used coffee grounds, which could still be transformed into a credible cup of coffee of far better quality than what they were brewing from dried ground acorns. The Polish guards had the right to inspect anything brought in or out of the compound by non-Americans. Some took a great delight in insisting these treasures carried by the maids be tipped to the ground, preferably over their boots.

Our social life was mostly limited to the compound, which was like a small town complete with schools, sick bay, post exchange and commissary, as well as clubs for both enlisted and officers. To relieve the tedium of such close quarters, there were outside recreational activities like cruises down the Rhine on Hitler's yacht, which was now in American hands. The unspoiled countryside was beautiful to sail through, and I had my first glimpse of tiered vineyards on the river bank. Even more fascinating was the large rock where Lorelei was purported to have sat combing her hair and luring sailors to their death.

With a staff of two in a small house, I had time on my hands. A neighbor told me that she was proposing to take a crash course in teaching through the Army Educational Service in order to open a Kindergarten for dependents' children. Up until now, my only training had been for a secretarial career, with the intention that I would end up marrying "the boss." Instead, I had fallen in love with a sailor. I welcomed this new opportunity to do something constructive. Once our training was completed, we were given the premises to open our school; Hela brought my son over for nursery sessions as I embarked on my new career path.

My husband's job in Frankfurt involved a lot of travel, which he declined to discuss. It was some time before I discovered why. He was a member of a unit that was in a covert contest between the Americans and Russians as to who could collect the most German scientists for the future space program. There were extra induce-ments to get them to America: They could take unlimited numbers of their family. To include their domestic staff, they married them off to uncles and cousins. My husband had the responsibility of completing this intricate paperwork. By this stage, all danger of Russian intervention was gone, so I was allowed to accompany my husband on the journey for the final signatures. This gave me the opportunity to see much more of the lush countryside of Germany than would have been ordinarily possible.

I had a more close encounter with the menace of Russia at that time. They did not wish to be friendly. We had the opportunity of a weekend visit to Berlin, which was a minimodel of Bremerhaven. All the Allies were represented there. What made me uneasy was the fact that to get there we had to travel many miles through the Rus-sian zone. My husband assured me that this would be no problem, but during the night there was a pounding on our compartment door. It was like a scene from a spy movie as Russian guards de-manded our travel papers. They seemed disappointed that they were in order.

Russians were an even heavier presence in Berlin where all the most historical sights were in their part of the city. I could not allow that to spoil the opportunity to visit the balcony from which Hitler had addressed his troops or the bunker where he had supposedly committed suicide. Not long after that, the Russians sealed up this moment of history, so we became part of the fortunate few who had actually had a visit.

Shortly after our return to Frankfurt, I learned another service wife lesson: Be prepared to depart at a moment's notice. The Berlin airlift began, and no one knew how it would end—the possibility loomed of another war. We wives began to pack some of our belong-ings and send them back to the States ahead of what might be a fast exit on our part. That did not happen, but when it was over, we did move. We were transferred from Frankfurt to Heidelberg. My husband's new job would be negotiating with a German company in nearby Mannheim, which had made a gadget for U-boats that the U.S. Navy now desired.

Moving to Heidelberg presented no problem for our precious Hela. It was only forty miles down the autobahn and still in the American zone. As part of our family, no questions would be asked. In Hei-delberg, we were expected to do our own home hunting from a list of properties. Since we were part of a large contingent of new arri-vals, we were numbered in priority and advised to make more than one choice as a safeguard against anyone ahead of us making the same claim.

Heidelberg was my first experience of a medieval town. I was charmed at the ancient architecture and the fact that it was bisected by a river. The residential areas that sloped down each side had splendid views. I hoped that we were going to be able to find our new home among them. After a discouraging tour of properties, we arrived at the gate of a large, two-apartment house reached by a steep set of steps from which one could have successfully made a bungee jump. The house was built into the hill, the incline so sharp that the back bedrooms were at ground level. There was no key available, but the people in the apartment upstairs were willing to show us their floor plan. There were even staff quarters on the top floor, which meant that Hela could have some privacy from us in the evening if she so chose. To our delight, when we assembled to declare our choice, the hillside position of the house had not attracted any of the other house hunters. It was ours.

My husband's new job threw me into entertaining in some style. The managing director of the German company he was dealing with had been at Oxford before the war and had an impeccable English accent. His wife spoke only German, so my growing vocabulary learned from Hela was put to good use. Food was still in short supply in Germany, so they appreciated our frequent dinner invitations.

Germany was close enough to England for me to make several visits back. Flying was still a novelty to me, and I felt very modern whipping over the Channel in this fashion. The glamor dissipated at Heathrow, which was a tiny village then compared to the travel city it has become. In the 1940s passengers were processed in a tent. It was still wonderful having time back in London, which, like the German cities I had seen, was very slowly getting back into peacetime mode.

The greatest danger for a service wife is to feel settled. We were really enjoying our time in Heidelberg, but in less than a year, my husband's orders came in for his next assignment. I could not complain—it was Florida, and there was an immediate movie image of palm trees, sea, and sand. The only problem was that this time I could not smuggle Hela along with us. It was a very sad parting. Eventually she returned to her home area, her husband came back from Russia a different man, and she wrote to say that life was very difficult.

Our return journey to the States was my first crossing of the Atlantic by plane. This was a U.S. Government–sponsored flight, which, unlike crossing the sea by ship, was very basic. We took our own refreshments on board. As yet there were no direct flights. This meant we had a six-hour stopover in the Azores, which was very disruptive for all the accompanying, small dependent children. There was a shorter stop at St. Johns, Newfoundland, before finally touching down at the air force base in Springfield, Massachusetts. From there on we traveled by train to New York, where my husband's usual pattern for going "home" took us to Chicago and thence south.

Our plan was to buy a car while we were on leave in Sesser to drive down to our new base in Key West. This purchase took more negotiating than we expected. The automobile industry had yet to fully recover from their war effort, and in 1949 cars were still in short supply in the United States. Our problem was finally resolved with the help of a cousin who had "connections." I was somewhat nervous of him because I had never before met a person who wore a gun in a holster under his arm. I was assured that it was more for show than use. I did not ever discover how much that helped us acquire a new 1949 Ford. Somewhat reminiscent of the situation that we had left behind in Germany, this car also came with a black market price.

I was very excited as we set off for Florida because I was now going to have the opportunity to see more of the United States. Differences began to appear as we crossed from Illinois into Kentucky where the larger houses were built of local golden stone. The red earth of Georgia was fascinating too because I had only seen black dirt before. The local dish of catfish and hushpuppies remains, to this day, one of my favorite meals.

I was not quite as charmed with the overnight accommodation that was close to the highways. In the late 1940s, the orange roofs of Howard Johnson's were barely beginning to appear. Some of the towns that we bypassed had hotels, but to find them would have taken up more time than we could now spare before my husband was due to report to his new station. Therefore, we had to settle for unplumbed, rickety wooden tourist cabins, mostly perched on stilts. The "office" at the end of the line was invariably decorated with flapping chenille spreads and string bags of pecans for sale. I did not realize that this simplistic architecture should have forecast what was ahead.

For the moment, my expectations were high as we crossed from Georgia into Florida. I rolled down the windows expecting to inhale the fragrance of orange blossom and recoiled at the stink of smudge pots coming from the citrus orchards. We had arrived in the middle of a cold snap. The Florida that I had expected from Betty Grable movies, which had shown coconut dangling palms and sparkling blue sea, did not unroll until we were much further south. Miami came up to expectation with lush looking hotels and shiny swimming pools, but there was no time to stop on our way down to the Keys.

Key West was still a sleepy little Southern town that did its best to cope with the winter visitors—us included because there was no Navy housing immediately available. We could not afford the one plush hotel and had to settle for a shabby room in a dubious looking lodging house. In the middle of the night I woke up to the sight of cockroaches creeping out of the cracked linoleum floor. I had yet to know they would be a constant problem in Florida. As far as I was concerned, then, there was no question of us staying another night. Next morning, we did manage to find something marginally better— a room with an extension of a balcony adapted by virtue of a two-burner stove balanced on a box, called the "kitchen." Like all service wives, I had no choice but to adjust to this change of scene that brought me from a spacious apartment complete with staff of two to these spartan surroundings.

Those comfortable, residential conditions in Germany would never be replaced, but our housing situation would get better. We were assigned quarters on the base at Boca Chica, a Naval Air Station on one of the chain of Keys. The Quonset huts that had been used as barracks in wartime had now been adapted into end-to-end housing. We had two tiny bedrooms, a minute kitchen, an equally small bathroom with shower, but a comfortable living room. Its only drawback was a black smudge on the wall, 18 inches high. This was the aftermath of a recent hurricane, and I was warned that in Florida, one should be prepared. Before the season even started, one stocked up on canned goods and candles and kept evacuation points pinned to the wall.

The compensation for such possible danger was living on a tropical island. I was enchanted; this base was landscaped with exotic and colorful vegetation. I had never been in such close proximity to date-bearing trees and pineapple palms. There was also an Olympic-sized pool; I felt like I was on a movie set. Downtown Key West was also a visual delight of boulevards edged with Poincianna trees, which gave echoes of dancing to the music of Glen Miller during the war.

In Florida, I finally became a real American housewife. Everything for our home was supplied by the U.S. Navy except for extras like a washing machine. We went downtown to buy one and an ironing board that would accompany me through the rest of my life. On the underside is pencilled its price, $6.25, and below it $119.75 for the washing machine—quite expensive given the level of salaries in

1949. Besides its electric wringer, mine had the extra sophistication of a hose for filling and emptying water!

Boca Chica is composed of coral and stood only a few inches above sea level. There were barren, deserted roads, which made a perfect place for me to learn to drive. A couple of times my back-up technique nearly foundered when I faltered dangerously close to a ditch, but it was all good training and I finally passed my test. Now that I was mobile I was able to utilize my teacher training. I applied and was accepted for the position of assistant in a civilian kindergarten in downtown Key West, eight miles away. My son went with me until he started grade school; then he was bused in and out from the base.

This kindergarten was very different from the drab premises that we had to adapt to in Germany. Classes were held in the open air on a wide porch or on the lawn of the large yard. My experiences reading stories to the children also proved different. I had to minister to mosquito bites and make sure they didn't get sunburned. On one occasion, they insisted that there was a snake under my chair. Having already been warned of such dangers on the base where there were rattlers and cottonmouth water moccasins, I had to accept that this was a possibility, but with the responsibility of a class of children, I needed to stay calm. I gently suggested that we all creep quietly away. Fortunately, when inspected, this one proved to be a harmless chicken snake.

Florida was, in many ways, like an enjoyable three-year holiday. We had the good fortune to suffer only from the fringes of a hurricane. Most days, we bathed in a beneficial sun. However, I could not have any regrets when my husband received his next set of orders; they were for London, England.

Except for an accent that had stayed valiantly British, a somewhat Americanized me returned to London more demanding of everything when it came to househunting. I insisted on central heating rather than the prevalent coal-fed fireplace in each room. Fortunately through a friend we heard of a large apartment that suited us. It even had maid's quarters, though by now this was no longer important to me. The luxury of a daily cleaning woman would suffice.

My son was enrolled in a British school, which called for a grey uniform edged in white braid, hardly the best choice for his age group, but he enjoyed everything that the school offered. I picked up on my life with friends and family as if I had never been away.

Such was the sensitivity of my husband's new job (all I knew about it was that the paperwork had to be shredded after use) that he was

investigated all the way back to his high school and the corner grocery where his mother had shopped. I gathered later that they had
also checked up on me; all of which led to the foolish assumption
that we might count on quite a few years in London.

We could not have arrived at a more exciting time. This was Coronation year and the city was a red, white, and blue galaxy of dec-
orations. The night before the ceremony at Westminster Abbey we
drove around London in our American automobile, which by its size
made it an item of curiosity. Massed crowds were already camping
out on the sidewalks, and someone yelled at us to turn on our radio
to find out if Hilary had yet conquered Everest. (He had.) On the
actual day of the coronation, we preferred to accept a neighbor's
invitation to watch the ceremony on television (still very much a
novelty in the mid-1950s) rather than return to London where all
the best vantage points to see the procession were already claimed.

My life in London, with its theaters, museums, and art galleries,
confirmed to me that I was a creature of a city that was irreplaceable
in the States, but my husband's life was in the U.S. Navy, and I had
to follow him. That did not stop me from being devastated when he
was ordered back to the States before his two-year tour in London
had been completed.

We assumed that it must be something very important in Charleston, South Carolina, to demand his almost immediate presence, but
when we arrived, my misery was compounded by the fact that he
had been brought back for the most mundane of administrative
jobs. The command at Charleston had the sense to recognize its
mistake. Within a couple of months we were on the move, though
not back to London. Our new destination was Great Lakes Naval
Training Station, situated just north of Chicago. At least I had the
compensation of being near a large city again. The extra bonus was
the fact that my best friend from Key West was already there with
her family. I was spared the fate of having to start a social life from
scratch, which is the usual problem for a service wife on a new base.

We were allocated base housing, which consisted of two-story ter-
races of unfurnished two- and three-bedroom houses in vast, well-
kept grounds. So, for the first time in ten years of married life, I was
required to buy more than a washing machine. The base had a mag-
nificent, well-stocked library, which enabled me to study the fact
and fiction relating to America's social history—a subject that has
always fascinated me. I read through Sinclair Lewis, Theodore Drei-
ser, Edna Ferber, F. Scott Fitzgerald—all new names to me as was
Jack Kennedy's *Profiles in Courage*. The theaters downtown were
equally wonderful. I saw Deborah Kerr in *Tea and Sympathy* and
Patty Duke in *The Bad Seed*.

None of this completely stopped me from being homesick for England. I needed to start saving for a visit and applied for the advertised job of assistant at the base kindergarten. They had another position vacant for which they felt I was qualified, so at the age of 29 I became the principal.

The challenge was to revitalize an ailing institution sliding into the red. With the help of an imaginative staff, the children were divided up with class names, which gave them the pride of identification. They started as "kittycats" and worked their way up through "puppydogs" and then to my kindergarten class, which were "bunny rabbits," where they were introduced to, among other things, classical musical movement. To my amusement, the macho boys took it on as happily as the girls.

As I began to meet more people at Great Lakes, I discovered there were quite a few war brides from various countries. We formed a club, which had the advantage of being able to use the school premises for meetings in the evening. I foolishly began to plan ahead, but instead I had to pack. My husband was going to sea on the aircraft carrier *Lake Champlain* out of Norfolk, Virginia. For once, a transfer was going to fall in with my plans. This ship would embark on the traditional summer midshipmen's Mediterranean cruise. Once I was settled in Norfolk, I was going to Europe, too. After a few days in London, as planned, my son and I joined my husband in Cannes, France, which was one of the ports of call. My enduring memory of this place is the sailors who came ashore intent on renting *pedallos*, which are small boats operated by bicycle-type pedals. They returned on them to circle the carrier like a swarm of bees.

Before I went back to England, my husband informed me that at the end of the cruise, his ship would not be returning to Norfolk but to Jacksonville, Florida, instead. For once, there would be no problem in finding housing as one of the sailors on the ship was offering his place to rent. The address, Sky Crest Drive, sounded exotic. In reality it was up a dusty, scrubby palmetto road that seemed to lead nowhere until it reached a small development of two-bedroom houses built in a clearing of the woods. This confused the resident wildlife; bears would stagger out into the road, while armadillos scuttled frantically across newly laid lawns.

With my husband at sea and my son adjusting to yet another school, I decided to return to teaching, this time in an old, established civilian school. That, combined with the fact that we were not living in naval housing, gave me my first taste of American civilian social life since I left Sesser. I was well established in the town by the time my husband's sea duty came to an end and was dreading the inevitable departure.

For once, my husband, who had by now reached the rank of chief warrant officer, had a choice. He could either go into the administrative offices of the base at Norfolk or to a government department in Washington, D.C. I favored the latter because I could see the potential of the useful, future contacts that could be built up for when he was ready to retire. He had already given twenty years to the Navy. The final decision was made by my husband who decided that he preferred the less frenetic atmosphere of Norfolk against a "headquarters" town. He also chose the final travel plans, which would allow our belongings to proceed to Virginia while we took a side trip to Illinois because he had not seen his parents for two years.

I was very sad as we prepared to leave Jacksonville. Each transfer and the subsequent adjustment were getting harder to take. My class at the school sang me out with "May You Always Walk in Sunshine." They were to be very unprophetic words.

My navy life ended June 6, 1959, in the hills of Tennessee. A drunk at the wheel of a truckload of swinging beef came round a hairpin bend on the wrong side of the road. My husband was killed, I was badly injured. Fortunately, my son was thrown from the car and suffered very little damage. We were rushed to the closest military hospital, which was in Fort Oglethorpe, Georgia.

Meanwhile, word had reached Jacksonville via the local radio station, and all my friends rallied round. One of my husband's superior officers was on vacation. He and his wife decided to change course and come to the hospital to see what they could do. The members of the war brides' club that I had joined in Jacksonville held an emergency meeting, then sent the chairman up to see me. Someone else tracked down my closest Navy friend with whom I had managed to share time at several bases.

The tragedy was headlined in the Chattanooga paper. A local, millionaire philanthropist had read the article and came to visit me at the hospital. Garrison Siskin, for whom a foundation and hospital are now named, exhibited his first act of kindness by installing an air conditioner in my room. Other readers of the article, including a war bride, came to visit. I was touched but not exactly able to be communicative. My broken jaw had been wired up, and the trunk of my body was wrapped in a cast. I was too doped up with pain killers to be aware of my husband's funeral, though I vaguely remember agreeing that the family in Illinois should make all the decisions. By now, my son David, who had to grow up very suddenly at the age of 13, was with them. He did the honors of receiving his father's flag-draped coffin, which came in by train. He stayed on there with the family while I recovered.

Six weeks later, I was released from hospital still in a cast and needed to be convenient to military medical assistance until it was removed. I had no home to return to for recuperation; my furniture was already in Norfolk awaiting further instruction. The chairman of the war brides' group invited me back to Jacksonville where I would have the backup of the U.S. Navy facilities until I was fit to travel. Devastated by what had happened, I had decided to go home to England after I collected my son from Sesser. The U.S. Navy shipped all my belongings on to England but do not think, dear reader, that I came out of this tragic experience a rich woman. I had no reason to have had any knowledge of American law. Up until then I had been cossetted in all aspects of life by the U.S. Navy. I was in no fit state to ask them for immediate legal advice. While they gave me plenty of practical backup, when it came to litigation I was on my own. A local lawyer in Chattanooga was suggested at a time when I was in no fit state to consider alternatives. This person turned out to be either very much in awe of or possibly payed off by the powerful team assembled by the opposition. All will now have to remain nameless because I had no strength of mind or support at that stage to do anything else. I accepted the first, very modest offer to settle the case and returned to England with my son.

Still in a protective body brace, I began house hunting in preparation for the arrival of my furniture, which the Navy was now shipping over to London. The prime need had to be a place with a kitchen large enough to take my American freezer, not easy since they were a novelty in the U.K. in the early 1960s. Settling down did not prove simple; I was far more American than I realized, and there were many times when I was tempted to give up and go back to the States.

By now though, my son was enrolled in the American school situated in the same Bushy Park where his father had once been involved in preparations for D Day. The boy did not need any further dislocation in his life. Once our belongings arrived and we were surrounded by familiar furniture, I worked hard at readapting.

Chapter Three

꼭 ⴰⵯⴻ ⴰⵯ

"Fast Forward": The Early 1980s and the Founding of TRACE (1986)

By the early 1980s, I had been married for many years to an Englishman who had lived and worked in the United States. Both of us at times wondered what we were doing back in England and decided it was a love of London that kept us here. We had frequent excuses to visit the States because my husband's sister was a war bride living in Cincinnati. This also gave me the opportunity to keep up with the many friends that I had gathered on my travels with the Navy.

My career path had changed course after I did a stint of teaching in an English prep school and found the system stifling after my experiences in America. I tried several different jobs, from sales to management and then public relations. My style of life was still very Americanized.

My son David was now married to an Australian, but they lived close by. Their two very British children had grown up to accept that Grandma baked cookies not biscuits, put gas instead of petrol in her car, and celebrated the Fourth of July with fireworks. They also enjoyed Thanksgiving as well as Christmas. Whether this eventually influenced my granddaughter, I do not know, but she chose to go over and find her American roots and is, at the time of this writing, working in Chicago.

Over the years, I had kept up correspondence with several war brides, particularly Brenda Hasty who had originally lived in Liverpool. She, like me, had been a founding member of the war brides' club formed in Jacksonville, Florida. She now resided in Arizona and wrote a column for her local newspaper. I envied her accomplishing this; writing was something that I had always wanted to do. I decided, now that I had retired, I could follow suit and attempt to get published.

I started with articles on subjects that caught my attention. These ranged from dog training through antiques and on to travel. They were accepted by several British magazines, but the greatest boost to my new career was when the *New York Times* published one of my pieces.

Brenda and I shared ambitions to do more, which evolved into a long distance collaboration for a TV series on war brides. Given our own experiences plus those of the many women with whom we both corresponded, there was no shortage of material. Since in London I had more access to television decision makers, it was agreed that I would get out and pitch.

Ignoring the fact that I had no television credits, I tried and ran the gamut of a long list of rejections. One producer softened her turndown with the suggestion that the story lines that centered on four main characters would make an interesting novel. We took her advice but found no equal enthusiasm from any publisher.

The situation showed no sign of improvement until, through a family connection, I was introduced to a prominent agent. His professional advice was either a hire ghostwriter or, since the book was based on fact, we should write it that way. We agreed and chose as a title, *Any Gum, Chum?*—a catchphrase associated with the World War II G.I. in the U.K. It was a constant question to them from the candy-rationed children. We prepared a proposal and a first chapter.

A publisher approved the idea, but the title was no longer recognizable in the current vocabulary. They requested a change. As any writer will concur, this is no simple matter and is akin to asking a parent to alter a child's name after the christening. Inspiration was in short supply until another friend of the family, Oscar Lerman, the late husband of Jackie Collins, encouraged me to pick a popular song of that period. My memory of the band playing "Sentimental Journey" as the brides' ships had pulled into New York offered the perfect choice.

With a deadline now for completion, transatlantic collaboration became difficult. We agreed that Brenda should concentrate on the research and I would assemble it into chapters. What we were yet to realize was that the delays we had encountered along the way were now going to work in our favor. Our publication date of 1984 would coincide with the fortieth anniversary of D Day.

Two television documentaries were also underway; both chose to feature how the British G.I. brides had fared after their arrival in the United States. One also made brief mention of some of the G.I. children who were left behind. This, combined with the publicity for *Sentimental Journey*, brought a mass of letters from people looking for help in finding their G.I. fathers. The television company asked if I would deal with them.

There were two reasons why I could. I had married an American serviceman, had lived in the States, and could give advice on the cultural differences between the countries; as important, I could empathize with this need to find the missing link. My mother had died when I was a baby; I knew what it was like to suffer an empty space. In 1986, those letter writers became founding members of Transatlantic Children's Enterprise (TRACE).

The idea was that I could give them some basic advice on how to start the search, and they could return for more suggestions or encouragement. I had no wish to change course and become a detective. I continued writing and would have other books published that did not relate to the World War II G.I. Inevitably though, there was one on the G.I.s' children begging to be written.

By then, TRACE had been in operation for some years; we had gathered a number of well-placed volunteers in the United States. Some were the brides who had been mentioned in the first book. At this stage, all the members were British because the U.K. was the only place where information about TRACE was available. Inquiries to the U.S. Embassy, advice columns in British newspapers and magazines, and the Citizens' Advice Bureaux (independent advice centers funded by local government with offices all over the U.K.) relating to G.I. fathers were all sent the address of TRACE.

The Salvation Army, which only deals with legitimate children seeking lost family, also began to offer TRACE as an alternative. Word got out to associate organizations dealing with adopted children whose fathers had been a G.I.s and they wrote for help. All this caused a great growth in membership.

In 1986, when TRACE began, there was yet to be the wide use of electronics that is now taken for granted. It was very much hunt and hope, either through local archives of U.S. military bases to try to pluck out a name or libraries with copies of U.S. telephone directories. Telephone inquiries could be approached if the person knew the town where their father lived, though, of course, it was now forty years later and there was little likelihood that he was still there. This was merely supposed to be the first step—a confirmation of where he was. We always cautioned about actually making the call; the shock could be dangerous after all this time, let alone unfair to his family who might know nothing about this wartime episode. Inevitably, a few were tempted to try, and several fathers went into instant denial. Such examples were quoted in the newsletter as a caution that this was a nonproductive way to start the search. It is worth recording though that many men seemed to be waiting for that phone call; "That's my Marsha!" was one delighted response. He, like many, longed to be found. One, in spite of many marriages, had had no other children, so at family gatherings he always produced his British baby's picture.

Most of the ex-G.I.s had no idea how to set about such a task as finding the children they left behind because the war had been their one international adventure. The few who had tried were rarely successful. The war and bombings had left many people displaced, and few had left forwarding addresses. Alternatively, as will be seen, men who tried came up against a wall of family secrecy that was impossible to dismantle.

Once it is officially confirmed that the G.I. still lives in his same hometown, one could write to the vehicle licensing department of that state for an up-to-date address. Then it is a simple matter of writing a tactfully worded letter on which we advise the sender's phone number to be a prominent feature. This often leads to an instant return call from the father. If he has died it is possible that someone in the family is aware of the child's existence and will respond. Alternatively, his American children, who may have been witness to parental quarrels relating to something Dad did in the war, may recognize the link and be glad. In the majority of cases this new half-sibling is welcomed into the family.

We get the occasional response, "What do you want?" People with two living, known parents cannot be expected to understand this need for identity. Some, to the sorrow of TRACE members, remain unconvinced of this and do not respond further. There has been one sad "leave us alone" letter from a widow who had responded favorably to the initial contact. The children of her marriage could not deal with the implications of a new sibling.

An early applicant to TRACE who contacted us on behalf of a friend was so quickly successful that she offered to do more to help. Thus, Sophia Byrne became our membership secretary. She spends a lot of time "mothering" the members. Between us, we have gradually found additional ways to advise them how to proceed. One great breakthrough was to discover that the Veterans' Administration offices in Washington, D.C., could, from a service identification number, disseminate the four most likely states where the G.I. had been inducted. For those who have this number, this shortens the search considerably.

If the clues are so few that the home state is unknown, one solution is to follow up on the ethnic origin suggested by the last name. For instance, anyone looking for a dad with a Scandinavian last name is advised to start their search in Minnesota or Michigan, and Italians are pointed toward New York or New Jersey. Basic as this may now sound, it often works.

Because many members were unsure how to start with such flimsy information, Sophia Byrne began to offer to write letters on their behalf. By this method, very early on she was able to achieve a very satisfactory string of successes. They included locating a G.I. who had been carrying a photograph of his British baby for more than forty years. Sophia also has an eagle eye for detail and was quick to spot the fact that we suddenly had two members looking for the same father. Sadly, he cannot be persuaded out of hiding, but at least, by joining TRACE, these two women have found each other.

We work on a voluntary basis and because we have other lives to lead, the paperwork must be kept down to a minimum. Sophia sends out application forms, which once filled in are forwarded to me. The information is transferred to an index card; the advice given is dated and added to the card for my records, and it is duplicated on the back of the application form and returned to Sophia. No other paperwork is kept or by now we both would have been overwhelmed by files.

People pay a small fee on joining. This goes to cover the cost of production and postage of a biannual newsletter to keep members up to date. Also included in it are any new avenues that members have discovered and are now willing to share. Equally important is the list of the latest successes. All members aspire to see their names in that column. The fee also defrays the expense of too many inquiries that do not include a stamped self-addressed envelope. It has also, in the past, contributed toward a yearly get-together in Southampton, Hampshire, organized by Pauline, one of our earliest members. Since she found her father, she has adopted his last name of Natividad. She was one of the more fortunate ones, with enough detail to find him without much difficulty.

There are some people who come to us with information as minimal as their father's first or last name. They are not expected to pay a fee but become honorary members until they are able to find out more. As will be seen on later pages, they soon discover that a little persistence can go a long way.

The one emotion that we prefer to avoid in the letters of inquiry is a tone of vengeance. Regardless of the story of their birth related by the mother, we encourage people to go into the search with an open mind. They must always consider the extraordinary circumstances under which their parents met, and that there is another story to be heard before making judgment. What seems like desertion by a father may not have been his choice. In some cases maternal grand-parents were responsible for ending many romances. In other cases, men came back after the war to find their child, only to come up empty handed, especially if the child had been adopted by a family member or put in an orphanage. Mother may by now be a sedate, grey-haired grandmother, but this does not preclude her from having been either a camp follower or a forward fifteen-year-old who deliberately made herself up to look older. This pertinent fact may not have been discovered by the G.I. until it was too late. It saddens me that as a consequence of such circumstances, many men re-ceived dishonorable discharges, which they did not deserve. Some women claimed they were raped. Since the punishment for this in the military could be as severe as the death penalty, such chances were not lightly taken. I fear that in many cases the claim has proved too handy an explanation for elderly ladies who do not wish to relive their racy pasts. As an example I can offer one particularly telling story. The mother claimed rape, and dumped her baby girl in a foundling home. Her daughter later found her, but she did not wish to acknowledge this child of mixed race. The daughter eventually discovered that her father had left her mother a note of apology. The encounter could be blamed more on an overindulgence of drink on both parents' parts than on violence, and we encouraged the daugh-ter to look for her father. She was successful and is now enclosed in a sister-to-sister wall of love around their shared father.

Difficult as it may have been due to wartime conditions, some G.I.s tried to claim their children. Erika J. of Koln, Germany, has now learned that her father came back to Germany to try to per-suade her mother to marry him. By this time the family had moved away from what had been the Russian zone where the two met. This was a period when leaving a forwarding address was not necessarily a good idea, so she was never found, nor has she found him yet.

There were a number of unscrupulous women who only had eyes for the generous G.I. marriage allowance and the possibility of in-creasing it by having a child. These women never had any intention of joining their husbands in the States. An example of such heart-lessness can be found in the Imperial War Museum in London as part of the World War II archives, in the form of an impassioned letter from a G.I. safely back home, begging for news of his baby son.

The question that I am always asked at the start of the search is, "How long will it take?" As becomes clear, there is no set answer, but the help that we receive from people in the States does hasten the process.

The best and most reliable source of official information has proven to be the National Personnel Records Center in St. Louis, Missouri. The great gap left by the fire of 1973 is gradually diminishing as more alternative sources are used; this, however, makes the search longer.

I could not complete this book without making a visit there. It is not obvious from the shiny, green glass building that it is minus the top sixth floor, which was the starting point of the fire. This has not been replaced. Charles Pellegrini, who graces many pages of this book, met me at reception. He is a tall, smiling man with a Zapata moustache and a warm handshake. His responsibilities as a management consultant reach beyond the letters that come in to him from Europeans looking for their American fathers. Once I was cleared with security, Charles led me to his office through an atrium that made it clear that this was a building dedicated to military business; flags of all the U.S. Reserve units were on display.

Charles's office was personalized with mementoes and photographs that illustrate that he is very much a family man. One can only surmise that this gives him a greater understanding of the need for people to find their full identity. Not that I would wish to infer that he goes beyond the bounds of duty; one of the center's information leaflets clearly states: "Limited information from the military personnel records is releasable to the general public *without the consent of the veteran or next-of-kin.* The type of information releasable is intended to strike a balance between the public's right to obtain information from Federal records, as outlined in the Freedom of Information act, and the veteran's right to privacy as defined by the Privacy act." The list of releasable items includes marital status, photograph, and last known address.

The time I felt I could take up at the center allowed for only a shortened demonstration of how the system worked. In spite of that, what I saw was impressive. This includes the letters that arrive directly in Charles's office marked "do not open in mail room" and the mass of correspondence that I saw being processed in the mail room. Not all relates to finding fathers; it is as diverse as inquiries on loan applications, retirement benefits, and lost service identification numbers.

An awesome seventy million files are housed in this building, which is a civil service facility; therefore economy is the operative word. This makes the cost of transferring all these records to computer too expensive to contemplate. The only electronic exercise involved is their location. This is punched up on a computer and followed by footwork, which is why I had been warned to wear flat shoes. There are 3,632,000 cubic feet of storage capacity within the building. The files are stacked on steel shelves in rows of cardboard boxes similar to those used to display apples in a supermarket. In this case they hold evidence of a person's service life. Such boxes are the most practical method of storage as well as being environmentally friendly; they are easily disposed of as they become battered by their constant use and replaced by a new identical model.

I was taken off for a demonstration of how the system works which led me past members of staff working at desks on each floor where in some cases they were still sifting through either charred pieces of paperwork salvaged from the fire or files that suffered water damage and were professionally dried out. This is no place to go into the details of the rescue of these documents, but one has to admire the ingenuity that led to so much being preserved.

All this activity made me appreciate the reason for delays in responses from the National Personnel Records Center and emphasized the importance of sending in as many background details as possible. The vision of a few people flicking through files was replaced by the enormity of the effort entailed by the staff there in responding to even the most simple of queries.

During the writing of this book, I had a speaking engagement in Plymouth, Devon, an area that had hosted so many of the American troops training for the invasion of France. While driving alongside those clean, now deserted beaches, one can feel the ghosts of men whose gravestones now make orderly white lines in the cemeteries of Normandy on the other side of the English Channel. Some of them left behind children who have visited their fathers' graves in France or in the Military Cemetery at Madingley in Cambridge, England. One woman took her son there every year of his childhood but did not tell him until he was forty that the visits had been to the grave of his father who was killed in an Air Force crash.

The greater majority of these European G.I. children are looking for fathers who survived the war. What has astonished me as I have gone through my notes are the large number of clues sent by people who have then not followed through by putting them on the application form that they are sent after the initial inquiry. One can only assume that they have a form-filling phobia, are lazy, or have assumed that for the modest membership fee, Transatlantic Children's Enterprise will act as their personal private investigator.

There was a growing preponderance of claims that the G.I.s being sought were from New York. I began to suspect that the mothers who had received mail from them assumed that the A.P.O. numbers followed by New York, N.Y. (the central point for distribution) indicated the G.I.s' hometown. This became even more apparent when I was sent copies of those letters. In them were clues that related to where they actually lived. This could also be deduced from the service number. In those days it was difficult to get much cooperation through military channels. This I am sure was partly due to the fact that there was and still is a natural tendency of men to protect men. To be fair though, on more than one occasion, there was a scrap of paper with an address tucked into the official envelope of rejection.

Our greatest asset in this search for fathers has always been volunteers in the States, especially if they served in the U.K. during the war. One of the earliest was Harold Ludwig. He also had the advantage of living in St. Louis, the home of the National Personnel Records Center. This allowed him to verify the fact that the fire in 1973 had actually happened and that many records that could have identified fathers were destroyed. Up until then, many of our members had assumed that this was an excuse to divert them. It was Harold who first showed us that there were other ways around this problem with a startling, early success. A member who joined in May 1991, courtesy of Harold, had the father's current address by June 1991. Harold was also willing to brave an errant G.I. at his front door if the G.I. lived reasonably within his area. A couple of times he had a bad reception and had to cut and run, but he had more hits than misses. He was also invaluable to people trying to locate fathers in units like his that had been stationed in Staffordshire, England.

One member of TRACE brought in a volunteer. She was a British service wife whose husband was transferred to a base in the States. There, she continued her search and during that time was befriended by Virginia Holden, a Gold Star sister from Pennsylvania whose brother was killed in the war. After Ann R. found her father, Virginia offered to continue to help TRACE, especially for those members searching within her home state and has achieved some notable successes.

At the start, we were rank amateurs in detective work, yet to discover the existence of associations attached to units that had served in World War II. However, when there was mention in the media of a well-known person who had been involved in a specific battle that connected with a G.I. father on our list, I wrote to him. Understandably, while I received charming letters back from the likes of Walter Cronkite and Dominick Dunne, who had both been in the Battle of the Bulge, neither, in the heat of battle, had time to remember the names of fellow servicemen.

As time went by, a few other groups were formed to help people find their G.I. fathers. Sometimes the founders were successful members of TRACE who now thought that they had the system licked and could therefore work independently of us. The pity is that by staying aloof there is a danger of people losing out, particularly if a father contacts one group and his child is a member of another group. A system of cross-referencing would be preferable.

An early group started on the initiative of Shirley McGlade in the Midlands brought benefits to everyone in a similar position to herself. It was called War Babes and attracted the attention of the Ralph Nader Association, who assisted them through a successful lawsuit against the U.S. National Archives and Records Administration (NARA), the Department of Defense (DoD), and the National Personnel Records Center (NPRC) which is a division of NARA. This led to a settlement on November 16, 1990, which contained essentially three provisions:

(1) the National Personnel Records (NPRC) will follow specified search procedures to look for records when a request for information about a veteran from a member of War Babes or "similarly situated individual" is received;

(2) the NPRC and DoD agree to disclose the city and state and date of whatever addresses are contained in the records of the G.I. being sought (if he is deceased they will release the entire address); and

(3) For members of War Babes or WWII children, the NPRC will forward a letter on your behalf to your father by certified mail, return receipt requested (meaning it only will be delivered if your father signs for it).

This could only help those with enough information for the authorities to comply with the above ruling. Even though the records could be forty years old, it was a starting point, and we have discovered over the years that these men do tend to return home to retire or, sadly, to be buried. This then provides a place for their European child to visit. Many have made long journeys to pay their respects.

What would be even more helpful to these searches would be if the various groups kept in touch with an exchange of information. (I recently discovered that there is another one in Iceland.) So far, they all seem to prefer to stay isolated from each other. Fortunately, a large number of people searching inadvertently benefit by belonging to more than one group.

Those who do not receive a reply to the letter sent on their behalf by the NPRC will at least know that their fathers are alive; then there are other ways to attempt to reach him, which is often where our American friends come in. For the rest of the G.I. children who could not fulfill the criteria set out by the U.S. Government after the lawsuit brought by War Babes, it is back to basics, trying to obtain more information. The problem is—how? By then, too many have already found that asking their mothers probing questions causes affronted arguments, denials, or tears. Such responses generally relate to loyalty to the marriage that followed the birth of the child, or social standing if the child had been born out of wedlock (this generation could be blighted by such a "mistake"). Such women hide behind a screen, saying "I can't remember" or "why do you want to bother?" There is almost an equal number who are curious as to what happened to that particular G.I. in the intervening years. In spite of that, no one—not even the mother, unless she has been in a similar position—can understand the need. "Half of me is missing" is the most constant cry of these children. This does not deter some mothers from taking their secret to the grave.

Those faced by such maternal silence try to find friends or family who knew their mothers in their youth. Younger family members might remember the G.I. from gifts of candy. This was how one was able to volunteer the nickname "Tex," which eventually would turn the key of a delighted father's door.

When a stepfather dies, the truth may come out in a coy but shocking confession from Mom: "Actually, dear, he wasn't your father." If the man had been loved, this turns grief into confusion; if he had been cruel (as has too often been the case) there is a sense of relief before confusion sets in. Some parents never tell the child of their adoption; on their death, the discovery of hidden papers presents other emotional problems. They are suddenly revealed to be different persona than they perceived themselves to be. Because of these complications, in many cases, I find myself acting as counselor before I can give any advice on searching.

In 1992 I finally persuaded a British publisher that there was a potential book in the case histories that were coming in. The book was to be dedicated to the G.I.s who had promised to come back for their British sweethearts but had been killed in the fighting in France. Some of their children have since visited their graves in Normandy and have been welcomed into their fathers' families. The case histories in that book ended with several pages of self-help advice for readers who might be about to begin the search. In spite of that, a large number chose to come directly to TRACE. I suspect that this was to compensate for their sense of isolation; they could join people in a similar position to themselves. One member put it most succinctly: "We are like a family—all with the same interest."

The physical presence of the book on a shelf worked its own magic. Wendy B., who had given up hope after her own prolonged and unsuccessful efforts, happened upon it in the library. As will be seen later, she has every reason to say now how completely it changed her life. Even more strange is that Martin L.'s wife hesitated over the purchase of the book for fear it would activate her husband's distress at his discovery that his father was an unnamed G.I. It was therefore some time before they discovered TRACE.

Another big change in the membership of TRACE began with a photograph. One of our successes was captured by the Associated Press. This was a charming picture of father and son, so alike with their receding white hair and identical glasses that they could have been twins. This reunion was reported in newspapers worldwide, and letters began to arrive from almost every country on the map.

Unfortunately, many assumed that the acronym TRACE represented an agency that could undertake international searches for missing fathers. We had to have a leaflet printed explaining that our knowledge was limited to assistance and advice relating to the United States. Only recently have I discovered that these people could possibly have been helped by the International Social Service organization, which has branches all over the world.

The largest number of inquiries came from Germany, the majority of whom dated back to the American occupation forces. This was familiar territory to me since I had been there at that time. Many of the dates of birth were proof of how little the nonfraternization order had been observed. This situation was more explicitly expressed by a later article in the German Press: as "Eine Kleine Armee."

I had been a witness to some of the romances that lifted the young women out of the miserable conditions and shortages that prevailed in postwar Germany. A tube of lipstick was a luxury that a G.I. could easily procure for his German girlfriend. But there was widespread, vociferous peer disapproval of women wearing makeup.

There was also, of course, the natural attraction of the young for the new and exotic, which the G.I. was, enemy or not. It was a repeat performance of what had happened in the U.K. These fresh, smartly dressed, healthy-looking young men brightened the drab suroundings for young women impatient to get on with their lives. The G.I.s came bearing gifts of candy, cigarettes, and canned goods with unknown but delicious contents. They brought a waft of exotica into the tightly contained communities still living by the strict rules imposed since the 1930s.

Where the G.I.s had met British girls in the blackout imposed by the potential of air raids, they now romanced the German girls in *bierkellers* or any other place that they might meet. The German women, the young in particular, were starving for male attention. One has to remember that large numbers of their men were now either dead or prisoners of war. The G.I.s brought some life to their drab social scene. This would be enhanced when American movies that had been forbidden became available for general viewing. Here was a chance to see beyond Germany, to identify with places that some of the G.I.s said they came from. These movies had a dazzling effect on young, impressionable minds.

One could disregard parental shaking of heads; there was the gloss of Hollywood for all to see. German girls became as enamored of the illusion as their British counterparts. Even if they did not yet have any chance of wearing the glamorous clothes seen on screen, they could start to be modern with the presents they received that sometimes came all the way from America! A heady mix of the natural rebelliousness of youth and a desperate need to now have a good time induced a large number to ignore warnings of danger ahead. For the most reckless, there was a price to pay. The shame of being an unmarried mother was as prevalent in the 1940s, 1950s, and early 1960s in Europe as elsewhere.

The only advantage for German children of G.I.s would be the greater local attention to records dating back to prewar days and still in operation. British mothers could prevaricate when it came to important details; they could hide behind the fact that they were away from home in uniform or that the family home had been bombed and there was nothing left. The German records, however, were there to be consulted.

Adopted, fostered, or kept within the family by an unmarried mother, the German children of these liaisons had, if mother was not forthcoming with information, recourse to the *Jugendampt* (comparable to a local Social Services office with the same responsibilities of overseeing and protecting the child). A visit to one of these places could reveal meticulous information on early history complete with the name of the G.I.—if it was known.

What comes over strongly in the letters that arrive from Germany and the rest of Europe is that the emotion is exactly the same as that of the original British members of TRACE. One of the most recent is a classic example: "I live in good conditions. To find my father or get some information about him is to find my identity." This is an important point. There are those in the United States whose immediate reaction is that these people are after money. I can assure such doubters that if we suspect that this is a motive it is made clear that we will not be helpful. What may be of interest to the reader is the fact that on more than one occasion it has been revealed that these European offspring exceed their fathers in income or ability. One father was pleasantly stunned during his first conversation with his son to hear that he not only had a thriving business in France but lived in a chateau. Another, listening to his concert pianist son playing for him in the music shop of a mall, was reduced to tears.

As eloquently stated in the letter above, the significance of this search is to find out one's identity, but certain revelations are unexpected. Searchers discover that they have links with American history; one member of TRACE is a distant relative of a past president, one can claim a well-known Western outlaw on the family tree, and many are from colonial and pioneer stock as well as from Native American connections.

Since information about TRACE crossed the English Channel, the mail has caused me to revise my school-learned knowledge of languages. I can cope with the sense of a letter in French, but my German is rusty from lack of practice, although my memories of the circumstances while I was there are useful. I can explain the reasons behind what appears to be desertion on the part of their fathers. Fortunately, to facilitate this, accurate translations of their letters and the replies were in the hands of Inge Gurr, originally from Munich who was my neighbor but has now returned to Germany.

Now that American forces have been in Europe since the end of World War II, there have been occasions when romances were interrupted by transfers to serve in other wars. Consequently, we are also advising people how to find men who may have become casualties in Korea or Viet Nam. Not all searchers are children of World War II veterans. The most up-to-date so far is someone looking for a member of the U.S. Air Force who passed through Germany on his way to the Gulf War. He was delighted to be found. Next on the agenda I am sure, will be an inquiry from Bosnia!

We are still ahead with acceptances as opposed to rejections. Some of those rejections come in the form of an immediate denial. This tends to evaporate after an explanatory letter accompanied by photographs showing the family likeness. The majority of fathers are delighted to be found; many have agonized and suffered great guilt over the child that they know they left in Europe. There are also some who have had no other children.

One has to accept that these men were in most cases, and still are, "small town boys." They have had no background on how to proceed with a search of international proportions. Whatever their memories, their children may have moved around, possibly as peripatetic as earlier Americans. For example, there is an ex-G.I. in Kentucky whose French son has visited this state several times in the hope of finding him. So far, all he has accomplished is membership in the "Combs cousinhood" and adoption by one of the members. He was working in New Caledonia but then moved to an even smaller island east of Madagascar.

The most satisfactory successes for me continue to be related to the men who had every intention of coming back for their sweethearts but became fatal casualties of World War II. Once this has been determined, the grave can be visited in the American war cemeteries in either England, France, or back in the States. There is nothing more real than reading that name off a stone. The next step is to find the father's family to learn something about him. This works both ways. The American family now at least has the compensation of a living link with their lost relative. In one wonderful case, the dead G.I.'s daughter found her father's twin brother.

While I see every success as a plus, I must admit to also favoring those where the ex-G.I. who has no other children receives a letter that makes him a father and grandfather in one go. All these men have much to feel proud about in their European children. Some have overcome unbelievable difficulties to find them as was recognized in a "thank you" letter from California: "I had no idea whatsoever that I had left a child in England and am sure glad that she didn't give up on me, it would have been my loss. I only hope other G.I.s find their children, it's a feeling beyond belief."

By now, many of these European children of G.I.s have visited the States, supposedly on vacation but often, I suspect, with the forlorn hope of finding their fathers by accident. When they discover the immense size of the country, they realize that this is an improbable shortcut. Some still clutch at what they see as a possible clue. I had a letter from a lady in Germany who said that she had heard there was a bookshop in St. Louis, where her father was from, that carried his name. I had to explain that this is a vast chain covering the United States. However, rather than completely demolish her hopes, I suggested that it might be worth a letter investigating the company history. We work on the premise that anything is possible, and sometimes it is!

Two German television programs in particular attract the person looking for a G.I. father; "*Bitte Melde Dich*" is a conduit for people displaced by the war who are now looking for lost relatives, and "Fliege" is a chat show run by a clergyman. Both include TRACE on their information sheets. They have been responsible for several successes. These in turn lead to televised interviews, especially if the G.I. dad comes over to meet his German family. This is then picked up by columns in newspapers and magazines, and inevitably our membership increases.

The credit for the most inquiries from one source still belongs to the advice column *The Mail on Sunday*, a British publication aimed at the middle-class market. A man wrote for advice on how to deal with the late discovery that his father was a G.I. They suggested TRACE, and Sophia Byrne, the membership secretary, was inundated with mail. Bryan was to find that his father had died, but he has friendly siblings.

By now, we have come to the conclusion that it is doubtful that we will ever be able to make an accurate assessment of the number of G.I. offspring in Europe since not all are interested in pursuing a search for their fathers. One person who approached me at the end of one of my talks on the subject merely wished to share with me that her husband was a G.I. baby. She was not looking for advice. They knew that his mother had put him in an orphanage. His loyalty to his adoptive parents precludes him from trying to find his American identity.

Some do not take their lack of background so calmly, and many are still only just making the discovery. This change of identity can be a shock; one woman who rang me from Germany very early one morning was in deep distress. Fortunately, she spoke good English so that I could extract some details and respond constructively. She had been put in a foster home at the age of two months and had grown up with little knowledge of her background. Now, she was confronted with the fact that her father was a nameless American pilot. I could only at that stage offer sympathy and suggestions as to how to possibly obtain more details. This has since happened; she knows his name and his home state of Ohio, and has a contact person there. Perhaps by the time this book is completed, I may be able to report her success.

In October of 1998, I had a similar phone call, from someone in England, but this was mixed with anger: "I am 53 years old and have just discovered that my father was a G.I." So far, she only knows a nickname, which was a quite common one among men in the U.S. Air Force. The date of her conception indicates that this G.I. was an early arrival. As a starting point, she has been advised to do some research into the units who came first. He and his nickname may show up on a group photograph or in a newspaper report.

The shock that these people suffer comes more from the unexpectedness of the information, not because the father is American. That he *is* American often confirms the unexplainable draw that they have felt for that country. Their devastation is due to the betrayal they feel either by the parents who may not have revealed they were adopted (it was not required at that time) or by their mother for never telling them the truth. There is now clarification of the fact that he or she is a dark-skinned child among blond siblings, or a victim of "father's" unexplained animosity. A deep-seated fear that questions would lead to total rejection also hold some back. This concern can stay in place throughout adulthood because they sense the problems it will raise.

This difficulty is greatest for those born during or at the end of World War II. Their mothers are getting old, some are dying, and there is a tendency for that generation to take their secrets to the grave. This can lead to an even greater shock for those who think they know who they are, until after their mother's death they come upon the proverbial well-hidden box of mementoes. Inside may only be a name at the end of a love letter or a scribble of a signature across a photograph, but it answers all the questions. One woman had treasured a tiny message from a man who might have had a premonition that he would not survive the war: "In case anything ever happens to me, always remember that I loved you better than anything in this world." Unusual as his first name is, there is no last one to accompany it. This means that there is not enough to find him . . . yet. But, as the following case histories will show, nothing is impossible. These will not appear in chronological order; no two searches take the same amount of time. While the majority of searchers share a sense of shock as they start, it will be noted that the more unusual the circumstances, the easier the cases are to unravel.

Chapter Four

"A Stranger to Myself"

The story of Mary L. J. of Wales is a perfect illustration of how children of G.I.s often found out that their parentage was not as it had been presented to them, and how that knowledge has haunted them through life. Mary writes:

> I discovered that my father was a G.I. through finding a well-hidden leather handbag. This was stuffed with hundreds of letters written by my father . . . I found them absolutely fascinating reading and most intriguing to a child who knew nothing of her father . . . I came to the bombshell letter which referred to the fact that I was half American. This had been written in Autumn 1945 in Southampton before he embarked on the *Queen Mary* for New York. One sentence remains etched in my memory: "Please tell little Mary, as soon as she is old enough, that she is half American. I desperately hope that she will get to the States—the best country in the world."

Mary was twelve when she made this discovery. She had her mother's maiden name, and now she felt that she had solved the mystery that surrounded her; she had a full identity.

> My first motivation was to tackle my mother (when my mother married my stepfather I was five, and I had to stay with my grandparents, visiting my mother at weekends). . . . I had no

idea of doing a search at twelve, but from the concerned, sup-
portive tone of my Dad's letters, I had no doubt that he would
come looking for me!! My mother was immensely relieved that
I had found out . . . was very forthcoming filling me in with all
the background details of their relationship. Unfortunately,
that was the last sensible conversation I've ever had with her;
future conversations were met with either "I can't remember"
or emotional "Please don't upset me at the moment."

When Mary reached her twenties, she realized that her romantic
fantasies concerning her father were not going to materialize. "Over
the years, I became increasingly aware that my father was constantly on my mind. It was a persistant niggle that one half of me
was one vast void. My children were growing; I needed to know about
my American background." Around this time, Mary happened upon
the Women's Institute magazine. The Women's Institute is a British
nationwide organization that offers opportunities for all women to
enjoy friendship, to learn, and to widen their horizons and gather
together to influence local, national, and international affairs. I am
on their list of speakers offering several subjects, the most popular
of which remains "G.I. Brides and G.I. Babies." In the issue of the
magazine that Mary found was a story of a TRACE success.

I was over the moon; at last I might get somewhere. But when
I received the application form, I realized that I had to have my
mother's cooperation but my father's memory was just too
painful; I had to let the matter drop so as to avoid causing
further pain and animosity. I did try looking for the letters although, unknown to me, they had been destroyed. . . . I put
the TRACE forms safely to one side hoping one day I might get
my mother to talk.

It was the the fiftieth anniversary celebrations of V.E. Day in 1995
that made Mary realize she was losing precious time: "I had made
the biggest mistake of my life in being over-sensitive to my mother's
feelings, as I had left it too late. I would probably never find my Dad
alive. I did nothing but howl every time I saw footage of brash young
G.I.s and the contrasting elderly U.S. veterans returning to visit old
service haunts . . . There was no question that even if my Dad had
died, I just had to know about him." Mary had her father's name
but was unsure of the spelling, which came from memory as she
was unable to refer back to those precious letters that had been
destroyed. For a while she tried different variations of the name.

It has been an endless round of letter writing and waiting for replies. . . . [T]he fact that people just don't bother to reply to tactfully worded requests for information despite International Reply coupons (which possibly they did not recognize) leaves one with a tremendous sense of uncertainty. Were the Carruthers/Caruthers contacted merely indifferent strangers or were they in fact family who did not want to know? There is no question of giving up; thankfully, there have been wonderful people who have shown incredible kindness and interest which has been a terrific boost to one's morale. I just can't begin to thank them all.

A letter arrived from Mary in November 1998 which reported the result of cross-cooperation between Philip Grinton, one of our U.S. helpers who had managed to identify Mary's father's unit, and Charles Pellegrini:

No wonder all previous enquiries proved futile. The spelling of his surname is Carothers! Now I have his full name, date of birth, and state of residence in '45. . . . The letter gave me an incredible high, especially when my son investigated a U.S. Death Record service on the Internet, and there was no record of his death. But once again—probably a familiar scenario to you, Pamela—that euphoric state has now plummeted to a stomach-churning state of uncertainty. I enclose a copy of the seven addresses which Philip sent me.

We discussed them in a long telelphone conversation. I discounted the one in Chicago and was not surprised that she had received a negative response from a gentleman in New Jersey. She was also the victim of an abusive response from someone in Oklahoma. This is often suspect, but the accent was so western that it was unlikely to be her father.

Then in December came the ecstatic phone call that I hope to eventually receive from all members of TRACE. This was tinged with sadness; the reason that her father had proved so difficult to find is because of ill health. He is living with his son in Tennessee near the Alabama border.

He had never forgotten her, and as Mary would discover, he had always carried her baby photograph in his wallet. A serious stroke had left him immobile but, to her delight, still communicative. She flew out to be with him at the end of December 1998. They caught up on the missing years, and when she telephoned her mother to tell her of her warm welcome from the whole family, Dad spoke to her, too.

Mary met her brother, who is as delighted as she to have a sibling. Coincidentally, both he and Mary's son are ministers, so there was a lot of comparative theological discussion. She discovered that her father had made her mother promise to send Mary to visit him. When he moved from the address she had, the letters were not forwarded. When the photograph he requested of Mary, age two, came back marked "unable to locate," her mother felt that they had been rejected and got on with her life. This may account for why in later years she discouraged Mary's attempts to find her father.

None of that matters now; Mary has been enveloped by her American family. She grasped the opportunity to include a visit back there in 1999 on a course emanating from the University of Wales in conjunction with the University of Wisconsin, which followed the trail of the Welsh farmers who emigrated there. Mary preceded this with a few days first with her father in Tennessee; she wants to make up for as much lost time as possible.

It was not until June 1991, when she had reason to examine her birth certificate, that Barbara C. of London became a member of this group, who have to make a psychological adjustment regarding their origins. She realized that there was a discrepancy between the date of her conception and the return of her British "father" from overseas after World War II. Her mother admitted that she had had a relationship with an American serviceman while her husband was away, which he appeared to have accepted on his return. It was, however, indisputable that the G.I. was Barbara's biological father.

Barbara lost several precious years trying to find the man her mother insisted was called "Will Willis." Neither I nor Philip Grinton could convince her that the first name was a nickname, not a shortened form of William. By the time she did accept this and started anew, it was too late. She discovered that her father's first name was indeed different, but sadly he was by now dead. She is trying to rebuild part of her persona from details supplied by her American half-sister, with whom she is now building a friendly relationship and who she hopes to meet.

Beth G., a psychologist in London, learned who she really was at the age of 45 while attending a family Christmas celebration: "my mother said that my youngest son was the image of my natural father when she knew him. I was stunned by the news. I had always thought that he was a Canadian soldier who was killed in action." Her mother was doing wartime duty in the British Air Force when she met this G.I. His is quite a common name, but she has volunteered that he was at pains to point out that it ended with an "e," which makes it marginally more distinctive. In spite of this, it was more practical to start the search via the Chelveston Air Base near Bedford where they met. The military historian that she approached sent a long list of groups, squadrons, and other units attached there at that time, including a fire fighting platoon and a military police company: "Philip Grinton has given me so many addresses to write to with no luck, so has Charles Pelligrini in St. Louis. He actually found three with the same name who were willing to accept me as their daughter when the V.A. (Veterans Adminstration) forwarded a letter but sadly, they were all Afro-American and I am a natural, blue-eyed blonde."

The search continues. Beth now receives e-mail from her father's genealogy group but so far it has not brought forward any new clues.

Josephine M. of London was 45 at the time that she learned that the man she thought was her real father had destroyed all the letters and photographs of her real father. "Three days before she died of cancer, my mother told me that my real father was an American that she had met and loved during the war who came from Steele, Missouri. Due to painkillers, she was unable to remember his name." When she asked her mother why she had not given her this information sooner, the poor lady said that she had been afraid that Josephine would not love her any more. She died shortly afterwards without being able to say anything further about the G.I. who, as Josephine was to discover, had been the one big love of her life.

Her mother at that time had been a married lady with a small step-son and an unhappy marital background. Like many other women with small children, during the war, they had been evacuated out of London to the safety of country towns. Their billet was close to a U.S. base, and given how the G.I.s constantly entertained local children, this may be how that romance began. As happened frequently in such cases, if the woman was married, the G.I.'s child took her married name and grew up assuming to be a full-fledged member of the family. Josephine confesses that when she first heard this revelation, she was very angry, "and sad that she had suffered so long without telling me, glad that I was not related to my step-father because he was so violent and a terrible need to find out more, but with so little to go on, that seemed impossible."

With the truth revealed, the rest of whom she had thought of as her family—children born to her mother and her husband on her return to London—now excluded Josephine from their unit. Her step-father died a year later, and there was little communication with her half-siblings until 1993 when a short note arrived from her youngest half-brother: "I found the enclosed at the bottom of one of Dad's tool chests, I thought the contents might possibly be of interest to you. The pencilled address appears to be in Mum's handwriting." What he had found was an old, badly worn, small brown leather purse containing a fragile old envelope on which was written, "Andrew Brumley R#3, Steele Mo. U.S.A."

> The first thing I did was cry; I realised now that I had a name and could begin to search. I was aware that I might be rejected, he might be dead, but most of all I was concerned that he might have been married before he met my mother and have a wife and family that could be really hurt if they found out. I felt that it would not be fair to spoil their last remaining years together for my sake. I had managed for 48 years, so I could carry on, which does not mean to say that I wanted to.

Josephine started immediately to find out how to obtain information about former U.S. military personnel by contacting the U.S. embassy in London. The embassy sent her a standard reply that included a list of organizations that might be useful: "their reply made me feel that the task in hand was impossible until I contacted TRACE. Sophie Byrne the Membership Secretary made me believe that I stood a chance of contacting my father."

With a known state, the most productive first try is with the vehicle licensing bureau; in this case, Josephine drew a blank, which she was warned could indicate that her father was dead. To balance that minus was one possible plus, when Charles Pellegrini of the National Personnel Records Center in St. Louis sent her a document on which was her father's service number, rank, and last known address. While it showed the same town, it listed route number 1.

> About that same time, Sophie rang to say that she had found a Willie Brumley on R#3 and gave me his telephone number. It took a week to pluck up enough courage to ring and when it did it just kept ringing. I decided to try again and just hold on till someone came to answer it. Finally a man who was clearly unhappy at speaking to me said that he didn't know anyone else with the name Brumley and promptly put the phone down. A shattering experience, simply because of the extreme emotions involved followed by a complete and utter depression.

Josephine may at this stage have indicated that she was ready to give up. What she did not realize was that, while we do not usually get this involved because we feel that members should undertake this themselves, Sophie has an unbelievable tenacity of purpose when she recognizes that someone is so close to completion. She applied her eagle eye to a map of that area and noticed it was very near the state line of Illinois. Without telling Josephine, for fear of raising her hopes, she decided to try a different direction:

> In late June 1995, Sophie rang me very excited and convinced she had found him in Granite City Illinois. This time I was very reluctant to ring for fear of disappointment but I would not let my husband or anyone else for that matter, ring. On 9th July, I rang and asked to speak to Andrew Brumley. She replied that she was his widow as he had died in 1979. I had great difficulty speaking as my hopes of finding him alive had been dashed but I managed to mumble my apologies for disturbing her; there was no way I could tell her of my existence now. As I began to replace the handset, she shouted down the phone, "Is this his daughter?" and to my astonishment, she told me how long they had all been waiting to hear from me. It appears that everyone knew about me and my Grandmother even had photos of me.

Josephine would quickly learn there was no fear of disrupting a marriage because, when her father had met his wife in 1950, he told her that he had a daughter. She discovered that he had been 36 when she was born and had wanted to send for them. To begin with, he compromised with gifts because, when he came out of service, the only job he could get was picking cotton at a dollar a day. Even with such limitations, he was determined to save up for the fare, an enormous sum of money for most in those days measured against the average wage.

Sadly, circumstances caught up with him; his brother was killed in a car crash, and he needed to help support his family. This becomes a classic piece of Americana of that period. Here was Andrew Brumley, one of thirteen children, the unmarried son who came back from the war and lived with Mom and who reached out for his fatherless nieces and nephews. In an attempt to improve his financial situation, he went out to work in California and did not give up on his dream to be reunited with his British love and child until the parcels he was sending her were returned.

At the start, Josephine's only contact was with her father's widow who, though confessing to limited movement and vision, was happy to chat on the telephone and fill in on details of the family, but she was protectively vague about their addresses or phone numbers.

Finally, as Josephine was beginning to despair of ever making some connection with her blood relatives, she became aware during one of these phone calls that a visitor was present and saw this as a chance to obtain some more definite and better information. This person provided the breakthrough she needed, including many telephone numbers, one of which turned out to be her father's sister. This in turn led her into the arms of an enormous crowd of loving relatives, all very anxious to meet her. "I wrote to them and sent photos of my family. One cousin sent me my first picture of my father and another of his grave and a map of Missouri showing where they all lived. Having made contact with these relatives, I decided to meet them so I rang to say that I was coming over and was overwhelmed with offers of hospitality."

Josephine—a Londoner, city bred—flew into the new world of small-town America with her husband. Waiting was a reception of arm-stretched relatives. As if she needed proof, one of her aunts had the photograph that her father had treasured; her mother holding her as a baby. On the back was written her name, her age, and her weight. "The visit was a great success and very emotional. They arranged a family reunion for Saturday 23rd. (I have the tee shirt to prove it.) We went to the cemetery first and then to the hall they had hired. We were showered with questions and presents."

Since her return to London, she has been engulfed by letters from almost every member of this extended family. Through them, she has been learning her family history, which includes the fact that on the maternal side they are related to the notorious outlaws the James brothers. The downside is the medical history that she has inherited. There are worrying details that will have to be watched. This underlines the most important reason why fathers need to be found.

One must add to this ending a few lines from the letter that Josephine sent our Sophie Byrne once her search was concluded: "it is all thanks to you, Sophia and I thought that you might like to share my news and happiness, with every fond regards and eternal gratitude." Sophie says that this is a letter that she will treasure forever.

It is sometimes difficult for me to be impartial when I read case histories that include cruelty exhibited to children who have had no say in their situation. They are tightly trapped by the fact that they know they are not allowed questions. Keith W. of Wolverhampton is representative of the secrecy preserved for the sake of domestic peace. The perceived philosophy that this is "good for the child" takes precedence over the emotional damage caused by such secrecy, that is, of course, if such people even recognize or care about the harm that their actions cause.

I have noticed that answering the questionnaires that provided the content for this book gave several people the opportunity to unload a lot of bad feelings. Keith, who had grown up under a strict regime, which included the fact that he was forced to accept the man who married his mother as his Dad, noted that: "I dare not question this but I knew from the age of 5 that something was different from how I was treated from my half-brothers and sister and the fact that I never stayed with their grandparents. I had very little confidence, no encouragement, no physical hugs, just a sheer existence." He finally discovered his true identity at the age of 50 by asking a sympathetic aunt. She told him that his father was a G.I. from California, but because she had had no reason to see his name written down, she gave it to him phonetically. This lends itself to being spelled several different ways, and one cannot be sure if it starts with a "k" or a "c." He has since discovered that his mother was only 16 at the time of her pregnancy; this was reported to his father's unit at Whittington Barracks, but it is doubtful that there is any official record. As will be seen in similar cases, to prevent local authority action, the G.I. was usually whisked away to another base. Meanwhile, Keith is working his way through lists of different possible spellings of his father's name.

Roger W. of Reading was in a similar situation inasmuch as he knew that there was doubt concerning his parentage from the arguments he overheard between his mother and the man to whom she was married. This was confusing because this person's name was on his birth certificate as his father. When he discovered that his mother was a married lady when he was conceived, he felt for the peace of the family that he should not ask questions but try to build on the relationship with his "father." This proved unsuccessful. The man was harboring such bitterness that he eventually wrote to a national newspaper about his experience of coming home from his war to find "a baby by a Yank." Roger then saw no reason not to try to establish his true identity.

His mother had kept the G.I.'s name and address and told Roger that his father had said that he had lots of sisters. This proved a useful clue and gave him hope that an ad in the hometown paper might reach one of them. It was seen by his father's widow, who told him that her husband had died in 1958. He took the chance of explaining who he was and hoped that this would not cause distress. To his joy, Roger received so favorable a reply that he and his wife were invited over for the annual family reunion in January 1996.

Whenever I see in the press or on television that there is an item relating to someone's search for a G.I. father, I anticipate from experience that the source of the story will be inundated with inquiries from people in a similar position. I therefore make it a practice to offer the address of TRACE as backup.

An interview on TVAM, one of the prime morning shows in the U.K., showed a lady discussing details of her success in finding her G.I. father and how she now hoped to meet him as soon as possible. Of course, they brought him from backstage for a reunion onscreen.

Brian A. of Lancashire was watching enviously. Until two years back, he had assumed he was part of a British family, though he could never understand why he harbored a strong feeling to go to America. Then someone gave his wife a book on genealogy; "the first thing we did was look at our birth certificates and we soon realised that mine had been registered 21 years after I was born." He was to discover that his original birth certificate stated that his father was unknown. His mother had reregistered him with her husband's name after she married. Brian's questions on the subject have now caused a family rift, but he now knows that he is half American and has a strong need to find his full identity.

He has managed to trace some friends and relatives who have filled him in on a little of his background, but it is not yet enough to proceed. He knows that his father was based in Freckleton Lancashire, but he knows only his first name, "Bill." One of his mother's friends volunteered the fact that they made up a foursome with two G.I.s on a night out in Blackpool. She claims that they were members of BAD 2 Company and also recollects that his G.I. father did write to his mother after that. She was then living in Preston. It was many years before it was discovered that these letters had been intercepted by the young woman's mother. (Many parents applied this illegal tactic to stop their daughters from getting involved with a G.I.)

One more fleeting clue pinpoints the fact that the other G.I. in that foursome, with the first name of Frank, had a Polish-sounding last name, the correct spelling of which is proving hard to establish. Two more firm pieces of information are that Frank was from Pennsylvania and that, while the foursome were dating, Frank had an accident that led to his finger being "pinned."

Brian has made contact with the secretary of the BAD 2 Association in the hope of putting an ad in their magazine that might be seen by his father or someone who can supply his correct name. So far, he has had little response and does wonder if the "male protection society" is operating on his father's behalf. What they may not realize is that this was a thwarted romance, not neglect on his father's part. He is now examining the possibility of someone recognizing these clues via the Internet.

Cynthia K. from Lincoinshire was 52 when, chauffeuring an aunt to a family wedding, the truth about herself was revealed:

> Since I was a small child I was told by my mother that when I was a few months old, her older sister took me and looked after me until I was 18 months old. I could never fully understand why my mother would let someone else take me especially when my "father" had been away at war for four years.
>
> There were many things in my growing up years that I have questioned but my mother's answers would make me think that I had been over-reacting.

Cynthia's mother died many years back; she has several siblings but has only ever discussed her doubts about her parenthood with one of them. They had both agreed that her fears were silly. However, coincidently, or possibly subconsciously, this was the sister who asked Cynthia to bring their aunt to the wedding.

> I had not seen my aunt for at least 25 years but this sister had kept in touch with her and I did know that whenever she had, my aunt always asked about me. When I rang to arrange to pick her up, my aunt was very emotional, kept telling me that I was special. When I asked her why, she said we would talk on the way to the wedding. I saw it as a chance to find out why she had taken me in as a baby. When she started to explain, I suddenly felt that I was going to find out something special about myself and asked her if my "father" was my real father. I think I took her by complete surprise because she then told me that in her teens, my mother had fallen in love with an American airman stationed at Coxhill during the war. She was with him for three years until he was transferred. My aunt has asked me not to tell anyone else, she says, "what is done cannot be changed."

Cynthia cannot accept this old-fashioned attitude; a piece of her identity is missing. Now that she has her father's name, she is determined to find him. Unfortunately, her aunt is not sure if he is from Iowa or Ohio; both states sounded similar to British ears at that time. There is so far one small plus, her father's best friend was from Chicago, though here again, this may not be exact information since G.I.s were known to claim the closest large town in preference to the small place that they actually came from. Still, it is a starting point.

Anger at this deception is fueling Cynthia's search, but she is concerned that age may have caught up with her father before she can find him. She has been put in touch with TRACE's contact Joan Peterson in Ohio in the hope that this is his home state and also has been given the name of one of our members for some emotional support. She understands because she too was a grown woman before she discovered that her father was a G.I. As a very determined lady, she will also offer the encouragement to keep Cynthia going.

All emotions go into overdrive when an adult discovers that he or she is a living case of mistaken identity. Martin L. of Hertfordshire suffered his first shock at the age of 34. On the death of his "mother," it was revealed that he was adopted. The problem was made worse by the fact his "brother" had found out first in their teenage years and, in an act of denial, without confiding in anyone else, had burned their relevant paperwork.

When confronted, their adoptive father, while sympathetic to the situation, admitted that he had agreed to the secrecy because it was his wife's wish to pretend both their sons were biologically theirs. Neither seemed to be concerned about the potential damage that this could do to either boy when the truth came out.

Devastated, Martin made an attempt to try to find his true identity via a copy of his birth certificate. This revealed only the maternal half; the space for his father's name was blank. All he could hope for now was that, if he found his natural mother, she might be able to fill him in.

As has been mentioned before, chance and luck can be equal players in these searches. Martin was to find both on his side. Driving out of town with his wife on a weekend break, they spotted the street name that had been on his birth certificate. The occupant of what had been his mother's house knew where she now lived. Martin sought her out and received a warm and apologetic reception. Social pressure of that time had been the reason she gave him up. She professed not to know the name of his father. He felt he could not give up, there had to be another way around this problem. This appeared more possible when he learned of a local historian who filled him in on some of the background of American men in the area, but it was not yet enough to get started.

Through this gentleman, Martin was invited to attend the 1990 Memorial Day Service at the U.S. military cemetery in Madingley,

Cambridge. He hoped that he might encounter some veterans there who could fill him in on his father. This did not occur, but a meeting with a woman who was also looking for her G.I. father would, in the long term, prove propitious.

For the next few years, Martin resigned himself to the fact that without his father's name, he had no hope of finding him. A friend, recognizing his frustration, had a contact with the Social Service office in his area who proved willing to give the case a try. This person had the authority to access records that would have been beyond Martin's knowledge or reach. He proved able to obtain the file from the National Adoption Society, who had arranged his placement. In it was the breakthrough—his father's name and service number.

Confusingly, while this file held letters in which his father professed the hope that the baby would be a boy, there was also one disclaiming all responsibility for him. This may explain why the natural mother was reluctant to pass on to Martin the name of the man who was his father.

While he was digesting this information and deciding how best to proceed, a call came from the British woman whom he had met at the U.S. cemetery some years back. She was a long-standing member of TRACE and suggested that he would benefit in making contact with us.

Martin reached me at the start of 1998 as I began this book, so his search ran parallel with its development. As he was a new member, rather than spend time on paperwork, we advised him by telephone, which he and his wife then followed up.

His father's name fitted alphabetically into the files that had been saved from the fire at the National Personnel Records Center, but sadly, Martin had lost his race with time. He was notified that his father had died in a freak accident as a comparatively young man. Enclosed was a cutting from his local paper reporting the incident. It was from Reading, Pennsylvania, so I advised writing a letter to the paper to see if they could provide either more details or an obituary notice.

From this, Martin discovered that his father was survived by two daughters, which may explain why he had been hopeful that Martin might be a boy. There was also mention of other relatives. To find out if they might still be in the area, I suggested writing another letter to the paper explaining the situation. They printed the story.

A letter arrived from a lady who was curious to know why, after all these years, there was someone looking for her late brother. I saw no reason now for Martin to hold back; this was his aunt, not a widow to upset, so she could be told the truth. The conclusion of this story comes in the words of Martin's wife, who did most of the letter writing on his behalf. It is dated October 10, 1998:

> We now have a photo of James Daley as a young soldier from Martin's aunt. Another letter arrived from his first cousin who said, "I was really excited to learn of your existence."
>
> That loving phrase made sense of it all, at long last, giving Martin a real sense of *belonging*. This man's son works at the "Reading Eagle," small world! I have asked that he try and trace the original photo in the newspaper story and any info on James' two daughters who are mentioned. The family are so keen to meet us, we go to Pennsylvania next year.
>
> You have been such a strength to us just by being at the end of the phone advising the next moves. We thank you.

There is one last observation to be added. In filling in on background, the American half of the family have answered an important question. Martin and Shirley now know that their twins come down from his father's side! In addition, on June 13, 1999 the *Reading Eagle* carried the story of Martin's arrival and a photograph of him with his two American sisters.

Chapter Five

"Things Can Only Get Better"

Attitude is the key to everything, and certainly one needs to be positive when embarking on a search of any kind. This is even more important when there is a marked absence of clues. The capacity for tenacity is another useful virtue. In spite of the years that I have been involved with these quests, I am still pleasantly astonished at what can be achieved.

Gillian S. of Wales is a perfect example. When she first approached TRACE in August of 1997, all she had was a first name of the G.I. father she had discovered. Gillian was receiving no cooperation from her mother who had only reluctantly admitted the father's first name to her when she was 32. With so little to go on and already a young mother herself, she did not think that she could give enough effort to a proper search. She knew that her father had been stationed in Staffordshire. Therefore, one of the first moves we suggested was that she contact Pat Plant, who will be mentioned later in the book. Pat's father had been in the same area, so there was a chance he might be able to provide some extra information. In this case, he was no help because Staffordshire was one of the British counties overrun by G.I.s prior to the invasion of France.

Gillian finally learned later in the search that there were three possible variations to her father's last name, then that her mother had been conscripted for war work in a munitions factory in the area where he was stationed. An uncle, who had been a teenager at the time, revealed that her father had tried to see her after she was born, but her mother had refused him. This uncle also remembered that her father had been a regular cigar smoker, but this was no real help. At that time the British were very impressed with the G.I.s and their cigars; they were to them a luxury reserved for rich men or an expensive treat enjoyed for Christmas. This would not help identify a G.I.; the majority smoked them as frequently as cigarettes.

Gillian concentrated her investigations around the area where her mother had worked. There she met a local historian who proved helpful in supplying background relating to both her parents. Unfortunately, it seemed impossible to break it down into detail for either of them enough to lead one to the other.

She tried coming at the problem from a different direction by procuring a list of the women who were at the Royal Ordnance Depot at Swynnerton in the hope that she could find someone who knew her mother and supply some details of the romance. It proved unmanageable: "there were so many thousands there (munitions workers) working round the clock. I have been in touch with the ministry of Defence at Carmathenshire from where I got her 'Record of Service,' but they do not have any cross-reference system to tell me what shifts etc that she worked and with whom. All I know is that she was at the 'Drake Hostel.' "

When she eventually joined TRACE, like everyone who only knows one's father's first name, she was made an honorary member until she was able to learn more. She was sent newsletters that kept her up to date with new developments and spurred Gillian on until she was able to convince her mother to reveal her father's last name. Perhaps until she saw other people's involvement through the newsletters this lady thought she was only offering her daughter a lost cause, though that is in doubt given her constant reaction: "I have no other proof of my father. I hope that perhaps on her death I might find some papers. I doubt it judging by her manner. I have asked her about my father on three separate occasions over thirty odd years and my husband has tried once, but her reaction is always the same, that it has *nothing to do with me.*"

This has all evidence of being a cop-out though the reason for this denial may be rage. Whatever happened between the man and woman who parented the child should not have any bearing on the relationship between the child and the father. Gillian, like many others, wants to hear his side of the story. In his case, he showed interest by trying to see her.

With a last name and a base, Gillian had somewhere to start. She also insisted that we now accept her application fee before sending her information to the National Personnel Records Center, though she was still unsure of the exact spelling of her father's last name.

The St. Louis office came up with several suggestions, but one name stood out from the rest. Gillian was advised to send this to Philip Grinton, who responded with news that she did not want.

Her father's details matched up to a gentleman who was now dead. Because there was still no definite proof that this was the correct spelling of the last name, Gillian needed to make sure that she did not have the wrong person. She was given the name of local newspapers to apply for copies of the obituary (a wonderful source of information when it comes to finding possible relatives who can then fill in on the father).

Her father's last name is a reasonably common one in the States, but Philip Grinton's help and interest in genealogy led to the discovery of an unusual middle name in the family background. This may prove a confirming clue. Meanwhile, Gillian noted that one of the journalists on the paper has the same last name as her father. We suggested that she make an appeal to him for help because some years back in a similar scenario the journalist took up the search and was successful. In this case, she will have to settle for family, but at least from them, she might finally learn something about her father. This is still an ongoing search because Gillian has yet to find the right man.

Tony Spencer of Essex vaguely remembers seeing his birth certificate and adoption papers when he was about 8. They were dated in the 1950s; even at this young age something did not quite ring true: "when I read your book, I was touched by Pauline Natividad's remarks about, 'liquid black eyes.' They are the eyes of my youngest son, Thomas and when my mother held him in her arms after his birth, she said, 'look at those eyes, they've been here before.' "

It was not until after his mother's death that Tony found a tactful way to question his well-loved stepfather. His answer confirmed that he had been born before his mother married this man. Revealing the truth gave the stepfather a great sense of relief; he had been concerned that Tony would reject him for keeping this lie over the years: "he told me that the story he had been given was that Mum had been raped by a G.I. I instinctively knew this was not the truth because of the loving way she looked at my son when he was born."

Unfortunately, several women hid behind the excuse of rape— hardly the heritage to hand on to the child. Also, at that time this was less likely to have happened. "Rape" was a word infrequently heard in polite society. That is not to deny there were those who tried, but they were in the minority. In the military it carried serious penalties. The prevailing custom that marriage came before bedtime held. In spite of that, there were women who would take chances as is evidenced in this book. In addition, few of the women of that time were used to socializing with the strong drink that the G.I.s could afford to offer. How much this was used with the intent of seduction will never be known. Certainly, it was often the end result, but this would have been due to lack of experience or stupidity more than crying "rape."

If the pregnant girlfriend then came looking for the G.I. who had caused the misfortune, it was not unknown for his friends to cover for him or a commanding officer to arrange a fast transfer, as Tony was to discover: "I found out that my father was a pilot and Mum used to go dancing in Hornchurch, Essex. She went one time after she was pregnant and his mates said he'd been sent away." This left open the question of why until an older aunt told Tony that his father was so conscience stricken by what had occurred that he came round to the family home to see what he could do: "my mother was out with me. My grandmother was very nasty to him and sent him away. It must have been after the war or very near the end of it. I felt elated that he had not abandoned us. I had felt hate and resentment before but I felt more contented after that."

Tony made a couple of attempts to find his father but he had little information to work on and time went by.

Suddenly, last year there was a notice in the "where are they now?" column of our local paper. It mentioned my date of birth, all my mother's Christian names and the fact that these people had my birth certificate [it was a treasure that his father had kept], letters and photographs.

After my trying International Directories and getting a few wrong numbers, the local paper mailed the source and when the telephone rang, it was my American niece on the line.

She would explain that sadly, Tony's father had died only two weeks previously. From the letters and papers that he had left, the family discovered for the first time that he had a British son and were determined to find him. These letters, which Tony was surprised to find came from his mother, gave them enough clues for him to be found.: "her letters to him were full of endearments. I don't know why they did not make it together. Perhaps she was scared. My grandmother also was a strong influence on her and ruled the whole family. I always remember my mother wearing a brooch of airmen's wings. Did my father give that to her?" The answer was probably yes. "As a young child, I had a coat that Mum said came from Canada." These relevant details in the father's papers, and the fact that he saved those letters, make the accusation of rape a nonsense. It bears all the evidence of a tender romance. What broke it up was proof of the indisputable power of parents at that time, especially mothers who were able to bring these relationships to an end with no regard to the consequences. One can justifiably suspect that this case represents a great number of people who have deliberately not been given the full facts of their background.

> My American niece told me that at his funeral, his mates said that he went back to England four times for us. He stayed in the Air Force a long while. [My guess is that this was partly for the opportunity of overseas duty and a chance to see his child.] Some of the above evidence certainly points to clandestine meetings and certainly accounts for the late registration of Tony's birth.
>
> I have a photograph of him in the 1960s looking very handsome. I wish he could have met his grandchildren.

We have several other illustrations of men who came back to try either to persuade the mother to join them in the States with the child or, at least, to let him share part of the child's life. In the majority of cases, the ex-girlfriend had gone on with the child into a new life, which she rarely wanted disrupted. This was especially true where an agreement had been reached that the child be adopted by the British husband.

A child of the mid-1960s in Germany knows that her father wanted to take her back to the States but had no legal standing. So far, in spite of consulting a CD-ROM listing of people with his name, she has had no success in finding him or any relations, but she has yet to give up.

Someone else equally determined was Wendy Bligh, who would not accept the fact that there were no files in the National Personnel Records Center in her father's name, especially since she had already gone through an extensive search to add his last name to the first.

Although Wendy was a child of the late 1950s she was still concerned that time was running out for her and she could not go to her grave without knowing who she really was. However, she started with no last name or service number, and it seemed impossible. She decided to consult her local Social Services department in the hope that they might have some relevant paperwork on her adoption. "Three weeks later, I had a phone call from them asking me to come in for an interview. The lady was a very good listener who took what little information I had: date of birth, where he was based and when. She did not promise anything but as I was adopted, said that there may be something related to me in Court records."

A month later the social worker was able to supply Wendy with her father's full name. Unfortunately, its initial brought it within the files that had been destroyed in the 1973 fire, so there was no point in applying to St. Louis. Undeterred, she started going through every Lempke in the U.S. phone books that were available, hoping that her father was still alive. In addition, she was in touch with a U.S. Air Force historian who was able to furnish lists of units that had been at the Manston base in 1957–1958. By the end of December 1995, she had come up with enough information to have it confirmed that her father was living in Ponte Vedra, Florida.

> Trying to compose myself, I dialed the number. "Hello" I said, "is that William?" "Yes" he said. "Well, this is Wendy." And he replied, "Yes, I know." I can't remember what else was said and I had rehearsed this, it just flew out of window. He took my address. We talked about the family for a few moments. I hung up first because I guess I was just in shock. "I did it." I kept saying to myself. A whole week passed with no contact, well, I thought, he has my address, he must intend to contact me but I could not wait any longer. I called him the following Sunday night.

The day after this call, Wendy received her first letter with photographs that put a face to the voice she had waited thirty-seven years to hear. Her concerns about her father's family were put to rest. She discovered that he had told his second wife on their second date that there was a child somewhere in England, but he did not know if he had left a son or a daughter.

Within three months, Wendy was on her way to Florida with tickets sent by her father:

> Got a big hug at the airport, this was important, the first hug from my Daddy in my whole life. My father's wife was very kind to me. The Union Jack and Stars and Stripes flew outside the front door the whole of my visit. On my bed was a white Teddy Bear with a red bow, that was such a touching gesture. I kind of felt like I was 5 years old again. My departure was tearful, I have never experienced such a rush of emotion and I didn't know how to deal with it.

The last word on this reunion comes from Wendy's father who sent a sweet note in March 1996: "A few lines of thanks for the wonderful week I spent with my daughter you did assist in locating me after all these years"—signed William T. Lempke.

Sharyn H. did not enjoy life with her stepfather and at a young age went to live with her grandparents. She was aware that her father was an American called Garold Adams but not the reasons why her mother had returned from Indiana within a year of her arrival as a war bride. She was subsequently divorced and from then on appeared to go into denial regarding the failure of her marriage. All she offered Sharyn were uncomplimentary comments about her American father.

When her father married again, he and his wife tried to keep in touch with Sharyn, but with no groundwork laid between them and the distance involved, she saw no point in accepting these overtures. Garold would try many times before accepting that she had dismissed him from her life. It would not be until the 1980s, when Sharyn, older and wiser, decided that she should make an effort to contact her father. She wrote to his last known address in Indiana but the letters were returned "undeliverable." She thought that she had missed her chance.

In 1996, she read a newspaper story about TRACE and made a new attempt with their advice. By now, her mother had given her her father's service number. This meant that he could be approached via the special affairs officer of the Veterans Administration office in Indiana who would redirect his mail or notify her if he was no longer alive. In Sharyn's case, her letter was forwarded to the V.A. office in Florida, where her father was now retired.

Garold's wife, Millie, was home alone when that letter arrived. By now, they had a family unit of children and grandchildren, and she admits now that "I could have burned it, he would never have known. My concern was how much this might affect our daughter who was a 'Daddy's girl' but he had not seen his British daughter since she was a few months old."

Sharyn came over in December 1997 to celebrate her birthday and Christmas with her father and his family, who immediately enclosed her into their circle.

I had the privilege of meeting Garold and his wife when they came over to Britain to visit Sharyn during the summer of 1998. They met a whole new branch of the family, which includes great-grandchildren for Garold. To fill Sharyn in on her American heritage, he brought documents and brown-edged photographs. The family history goes back to the seventeenth century arrival in Virginia and qualified Sharyn of Kent to be a colonial dame as well as a Daughter of the American Revolution. More important to her at that moment was having her Dad. Sadly, he has since died.

Diana Hildebrandt in Eckeinfoerde, Germany, whose story has been translated by Inge Gurr, was born in 1965. She is a very enterprising and resourceful young woman. In 1979, rummaging through her mother's things as many children do, she found some old letters and a printed engagement announcement with a G.I.'s name that did not match the signature on the letters. What did seem possible was that the G.I. who signed those letters was her father, which seemed thrilling.

Her mother, now married to a man who appears not to have wanted this old news raked over, was unresponsive. Diana was on her own. She wrote to the address that she had found but did not receive a reply. Determined not to give up, she approached an uncle and her mother's best friend for more information. From this, she was able to piece together her father's name, service number and home state.

Confident that she now had enough to get going, she did some research, which produced the address of the U.S. Army Enlisted Records. They suggested she try another address, the facility of which suggested yet another. For five years she went around in circles, and by 1988 she gave up and concentrated on getting married and starting a family.

Her hopes were resuscitated in 1993 when she saw on the German TV program "Bitte Melde Dich" the address of TRACE and sent us the information that she had. By then, we had learned how a G.I.'s homestate could be determined by the first three digits of a service number. Diana's father's number was from one of three states. Since her father had done his time in Service in the 1960s, the motor vehicle department in each state was the more obvious route than the Veterans Administration. We also suggested that she take a chance and try his name at random in a few more of the more well-known towns in those states. Improbable as this may seem, it has worked more than once.

Sadly, it did not work in this case. The name was reasonably common, so it needed confirmation with a town, which Diana did not have. She had yet to discover that he had a distinctive middle name, which would solve the problem. Determined not to give up, she wrote to President Clinton. His press office sent her a new address to try. They responded with a questionnaire and an offer to forward a letter to her father, which by federal law had to be left unsealed.

This reached her father in Mississippi, and he answered immediately. In August 1996, she flew out to meet him and her new family, which included her grandmother. She was totally accepted by them all.

This seems to be the place to put in a good word for the motor vehicle departments in each state. Their information is in the public domain, and they have proved very helpful, especially prior to the accessibility of electronics. Some states like Texas, Virginia, and California appear to have withdrawn from issuing updates on addresses because of unpleasant consequences unrelated to father finding. As will be seen, we have now learned from a member that they will, however, like the Veterans' Administration, forward an unsealed letter.

This information, learned by the persistence of Melanie Powell of Suffolk, has now been shared with all members via the TRACE newsletter. As a 1960s baby, the first advantage in her search had been to find that the National Personnel Records Center had a copy of her father's files. But she was advised by them that he had died. His last known address indicated that he had left family in California, which included sons. This made it easier since they would have his last name.

Knowing the difficulty with the motor vehicle department in California, she wrote and asked them how she might contact her half-brothers. This would involve a fee of $5.00 for cross-referencing information. They sent her a form with space for an explanation as to why she wished to make contact. It would be up to them to respond.

Melanie then waited for the slow grind of official channels, but it produced a letter from her brothers:

> They said that they had heard from the Department of Vehicles that I claimed to be their half-sister and if this were true they would welcome me with open arms but they wanted to be absolutely sure of all the information before they informed the rest of the family. . . . They asked me to tell them what my mother had told me about my father, so I wrote and explained that my Mum had died very young but I would tell them what I knew about him.

After waiting on tenderhooks for some weeks, a reply came back from her father's widow—a very sensible and tolerant lady, kind enough to send photographs.

> It was beautiful, she was so wonderful. When I looked at the picture of my Dad there was a remarkable resemblance between him and my oldest son. His wife asked me to write back and ask lots of things about my Dad. She also said I need to know my brothers and sisters. I can't believe how lucky I am.

She could have been so different. She told me that she loved my Dad very much and that he was only human and everybody made mistakes. She said that she would love any child of his and hopes that I will go over one day and meet my brothers and sisters.

In September 1998, Melanie's dream came true and I received an ecstatic letter:

> I wanted to let you know that I met my Dad's wife and two brothers and two sisters. It was so wonderful, everybody made me feel so loved.
>
> I found out all about my Dad and I now have lots of photos of him. My Dad's wife is a wonderful woman. She told me all about him. So, even though I will never meet him [he died of lung cancer in 1992] I feel know so much.
>
> Tell other members in the next newsletter, never give up. I now have a whole new family and feel very lucky that my story had a happy ending. June [her father's wife] is truly a wonderful lady.

Not all wives or widows prove this cooperative, as Kathy B. in Shaftesbury was to find out. Her story started when she was jolted by the content of a row between the two people that she thought were her parents. After that parental argument, Kathy persuaded her mother to tell her the truth and discovered that she was the result of a three-week affair with a G.I. in early 1945 prior to him being posted to Germany:

> I had always felt different to my brothers and sisters as I am taller, darker-skinned and more shy than the rest of the family. They all have blue eyes, mine are green . . . All I had to go on in my efforts to find my real father was his name, his nickname, the fact he was very tall, his home state and the fact he was married with three children. I was torn between upsetting Mother and "Dad" to start the search and of course, was concerned about ruining a possibly happy marriage which my father may have. I was desperate to find my roots, to know the other half of me.

Because of these doubts, Kathy's search was sporadic. She would go for years doing nothing, then have another try, come up against a dead end, and give up for a while.

During the course of these periodic attempts, I had tried all the normal sources. However the American Forces Records office [St. Louis] had apparently had a fire. The Salvation Army said I was illegitimate and they could not help. [This has always been their policy but now they send such enquiries to TRACE.] I also tried a Private Detective in America without success.

Two years ago, at the age of 50 having definitely decided to give up my search, I was with my young nephew who was looking for some books on wildlife. While he was choosing, I browsed around and found myself drawn to the top shelf of books in the third gangway. I pulled out a book at random and held it in disbelief. My hands were trembling. Here were stories of people just like me. Suddenly, I was not alone. I read that book over and over again.

After reading *Bye Bye Baby*, Kathy joined TRACE. We advised her, as she had the name of her father's state, to write to the motor vehicle department. She received back the address of a man with the same name, but it was followed by "Jr.": "the height was the same but he was only 56, could this be my brother? I wrote to the address given and told him of my search for a man I had never met, without giving too much away. I gave him details of my father that only he would know if indeed, he was my brother."

After four weeks, Kathy's phone rang in the middle of the night, and an American voice asked why she was searching for this man. She admitted that she was looking for her father. After a shocked silence, she was asked to explain more. But, at this stage, she insisted on asking if she had found the right man and learned that she was talking to her brother, who now told her that their father was alive: "the fact that he had told his children of his wartime nickname and that he had been stationed in Bournemouth confirmed to them that I had found my father."

While Kathy agonized over whether she had done the right thing by revealing all of this, the family in America needed time to digest this unexpected disclosure and discuss it with their father. A week later there was a phone call from another member of the family expressing delight at having an English half-sister. From then on, through a series of more calls and letters, she learned about their shared heritage; the reason for her dark skin was because she was half Cherokee.

I had been given my father's phone number by one of my sisters but decided to wait a few months before telephoning him to let him digest the enormity of the situation. One evening, I just went to the telephone and dialed. Nothing could have prepared me for this moment. It seemed to ring forever then, suddenly my father said, "Hello." In a conversation I can never forget, I spoke through tears. He asked if Mum was still alive and to say "Hi" for him.

Everything indicated that she was going to be made very welcome, so Kathy started to plan the holiday of a lifetime. She suddenly had a large family, who were spread out in several places in the United States, and most important of all her father. He now lived in California with his second wife. He would be the most important point on her itinerary.

Just before she left, a bombshell dropped. Her father did not now want to see her; his wife could not accept the situation and this was causing disagreement between them. The last thing Kathy wanted to do was make trouble between her father and his wife, so with a heavy heart, she had to accept his decision. This did not change her travel plans dramatically since she was also going to visit her father's sister who lived near him in California and was anxious to meet her, but her first stop was on the east coast.

When the plane landed, I could see my sister's face. She looked so like me, I dropped my case and ran and we hugged. We had an immediate affinity. We stayed with her for a wonderful week before I left to meet my brother. While staying with him, he drove me in a truck to the spot where his family had lived before my father went into the services. The house was just a ruined shack but I collected some large fir cones that were scattered around to bring home.

Kathy and her husband did the rounds of all the family in the area; then it was out west to her aunt:

She was extremely distressed that my father had refused to see me. We spent four days and nights talking endlessly about him. My aunt tried to persuade me to go tap on his door. I did not wish to upset him, or worse have the door slammed in my face. The day before I was due to go home, I felt I might regret it for the rest of my life if being so close, I left without seeing him.

Kathy and her husband drove the short distance between her aunt and father's home and parked close by. She sat in the car trying to deal with the fact that there was now just a door between her and her father.

I was shaking with fear and anticipation. It was decided that it would be best for my husband to tap on the door and see how the land lay. He seemed to be gone ages. Although I am not a religious person, I put my hands together and prayed. The next thing I knew, my husband was back to tell me that my father was coming. I jumped out of the car but my legs were like jelly. This tall, beautiful old man was shuffling towards me. His two huge arms came up to greet me and I held my father for the first time. He had a camera and he called to the postman to, "come take a picture of my daughter from England." We had only 20 minutes together (his wife had gone shopping) but it was so precious. I told him I loved him, he said he loved me and that he had always wondered about me. I left him clutching my photo and promised in future to pass on messages to him through my sisters (his daughters) rather than upset his wife. I am now a whole person instead of half of one and my life will never be the same again.

The situation of Claus Samen of Neumarkt/Opf, Germany, provides a link between this chapter and the next. He is a child of the 1950s; his father was a Korean vet. Claus knew his father's name, number, and home state, so the situation looked promising. Sadly, he discovered that his father had died in 1984, but his investigations revealed that he had four brothers. He hoped to find at least one of them who could tell him something about the father they shared.

So far, all he has been able to obtain is the location of his father's grave. There has been no further response to other questions. In the hope of meeting his family to establish that his need to know was emotional and not financial, he went to Missouri. He could not trace any of his brothers, but the owner of the funeral home proved sympathetic: "he showed me the grave of my father. Although I did not know my father it was a very hard moment for me. It was a 'Hello' and a 'Farewell' at the same time. It was my duty to bring some flowers."

Dad of Sharyn H. came to England to meet his grandchildren and great grandchildren.

The five grandchildren of Teresa M. in Ireland have the same color hair as their reclusive great grandpa.

Chris E. with his father and brothers—which one is the Brit?

William S. with his father and father's wife at a memorial to a battle in Belgium.

Anita V. wearing her father's medals.

Don W. trying out a .22 Magnum with Dad. Note the matching profiles.

Bill de Quick with his siblings in Utah.

Finally, Mary J. with her father.

A TRACE get-together in 1998. From left to right: Sandy P. (holding her American passport), Norma Jean Clarke-McCloud (in white shirt), Pamela Winfield (in checked jacket and striped scarf), Philip Grinton (tallest man), organizer Pauline Natividad (holding small American flag), and Linda Gunn-Russo (in stars and stripes dress).

Franklin, Pamela, Norma, and Franklin's wife meeting in London.

Chapter Six

Rejection Comes in Various Forms

After all these years of examining application forms and giving advice or encouragement on the telephone, one soon begins to recognize that fear of rejection is why many drag out their search. As more than one of us will testify, in our continuous roles as surrogate mothers, when we suspect deliberate delay, that person will receive sharp words from either Sophia Byrne or me. They have to understand that there is no longer any time to wait and hope that they will eventually be found by their fathers; they have to keep at it.

It is still very frustrating to know that those who have enough clues to achieve a quick success choose to fail or falter. This especially applies to German members who send files of papers with valuable information, then do not even respond by filling in the application form. If nothing else, it leaves TRACE, which operates on a tight budget, with the expense of return postage or a feeling of guilt if the stuff is not returned.

In all the newsletters I try to emphasize that speed is of the essence and illustrate this with reports of fathers who have been missed only by months or weeks. Almost worse is if the father is found and is by now too frail or ill to communicate. If each newsletter motivates at least one sluggish member back onstream, it is more than worthwile.

This question of rejection is even more sad if the mother married the G.I. father, who thought that his European marriage would not be considered valid in the United States. She may assume that it was a legal binding contract, but this does not necessarily follow. What the G.I. may have seen as a matter of expedience was mistaken by the starry-eyed girlfriend as an act of love. Some men are not caught out in their deception until approached by their child.

Especially suspect are those men who did not have prior approval for the marriage from their commanding officers. They knew that an official application would have opened up their records for an examination, which might have revealed a dependent wife and possibly children. Some circumnavigated this discovery by encouraging a civil ceremony and lying on the paperwork. There were also those who had an administrative cohort with whom they could connive.

A perfect illustration of this has come to light during the writing of this book. In this case, the G.I. in England appears to have had a sympathetic associate in the office who was able to produce for him the clean, dependent-free record that was necessary for a church wedding, when in fact there was a wife and children back in the States. This "adjustment" was compounded when the marriage failed. He sent "official" divorce papers plus an agreement for the child of that union to be adopted by his ex-wife's new husband. It was not until that son was older and applied, as would have been his right, for U.S. citizenship, that the discrepancy was discovered. The G.I. father is no longer alive, so the questions as to what motivated him to perform this charade cannot be answered.

Some of these men simply resorted to excuses for what was causing the expected marriage to be delayed. Doris P. in Berlin is the offspring of such a G.I. He had a long-term relationship with her mother, constantly blaming the delay of setting a date for the ceremony on the fact that he could not assemble the correct paperwork: "My mother went to the Priest for help and he discovered from the Authorities that my father was already married. She broke off the relationship but he continued to try to see her and me."

Given this strong interest in her, Doris assumed that her father would be pleased to be found. She was able to get details of his last known address from the office of the *Jugendampt*. Her letter was returned marked "unknown," which indicated that he had moved. We advised her to try the motor vehicle department of the state that supplied his current address. The letters to him there were ignored.

As her father-in-law was going to the States on business, Doris asked him to try a phone call on her behalf. The G.I. admitted that he was her father but wanted to be left alone. Doris was so distressed by the rejection that she joined a self-help group to cope with her situation. They tried on her behalf. The father's reply stated that he had no interest in knowing her. Sadly, she has now given up.

Carole R. of Bedford was not prepared to give up without a final try. She first found her father's name when she needed her baptism certificate. On it he was listed with a "foreign sounding" name, something that would have been unusual at that time in the area where she was born. She questioned relatives and learned a little more, but it was not until she finally persuaded her mother to fill her in that she would discover that there were three possible variations on the spelling of her father's name. This would make him harder to find.

In 1991, she joined TRACE and was advised to try the locator column of the *Army Times*; this, with the *Air Force Times* and *Navy Times*, was a publication used extensively and with some success to find G.I.s in the early days before electronics. Her father's cousin saw it and responded. When he learned who she was, he made her welcome. More important, she learned that her father was alive.

Once she had details of his unit, we suggested contacting Philip Grinton who was able to trace him after applying for payroll records from the National Personnel Records Center. From then on Carole proceeded with caution; she did not wish to disrupt her father's domestic life. A letter was sent via the special affairs officer of the Veterans Administration in his home state. Her father denied paternity, insisting that he had taken adequate precautions, but this did not tie in with the fact that his name was on her baptism records.

In the hope that, if he actually saw her he might recognize the truth, Carole went to the States and called at his door. With an angry wife shouting behind him, the G.I. repeated his denial of paternity. Carole can now only be comforted by the fact that she tried; she has actually seen him and heard his voice. But she feels that the only real way to close the door on this is with a DNA test. She is not yet sure if she wishes to follow this path.

Paula P. of Shropshire found out that she was half American when she was small and asked where her other set of grandparents lived: "When I was told that they were in U.S.A. I was pleased as I was mad about cowboys and thought that my father might be one (in Ohio!). I had no proof that he was my father, just Mum's word of which there was no cause to disbelieve."

Paula did not start searching seriously until her children were grown; then she began to be concerned that time was not on her side:

I suppose, deep down, I was afraid of rejection; Mum had built such a nice picture I didn't really want to burst the bubble. As he has now never replied to my letters and photo, it's deflated just a little but I shall still carry on although, it's a bit awkward not knowing if his wife and family know about me. I wouldn't like to rock the boat in any way (but a daughter of 52 would probably capsize it).

The father of Christina H. of Schorndorf stood in front of the Consulate of the United States in Stuttgart and signed his acknowledgment of paternity. Therefore, "there is always a little part of me that is waiting and hoping." To date though, she has had to suffer extreme disappointment. While on his letter of declaration he left enough details to be found, such as his service number which allowed him to be located in 1982, he is not responding either to direct mail or her letter via the Veterans Administration office in his state. This is very frustrating, but she feels that they may share a sense of rejection. Her grandmother took charge after she was born and made it clear that it was wrong to ask questions about her father, but, she said, "I know that my father paid money for me until I was 18 years old. Maybe he also did write and my grandmother took the letters away. She lived her life by very strict rules and I did not start searching for my father until she died."

Christina recognizes that her father, having made some original attempts to contact her and being thwarted, may now not want to risk further disappointment. She also realizes that he may now have a new life with a wife who does not care to be reminded of what went before. Meanwhile, she is left in limbo: "I still wish to know something about my father. Who is he? What kind of person is he? It is still very important to me. I have to deal with this anger and sadness, there is always a little part in me which is waiting and hoping."

Christina has since received a small bonus from her mother in the shape of a tiny parcel: "some old pictures of her and my father. It was very exciting to look at a photograph with me as a baby and my father holding me in his arms. A great feeling."

Since Christina knows her father's home address, I have suggested that she find someone like a minister to intercede on her behalf.

Iris T. of Aalen, Germany, has been accepted by all her family but the most important member—her father. She was very excited when at the age of 5 she learned that she had an American father. She even has his dog tags and medals, which were left behind at his girlfriend's home when he was stationed there in the late 1950s.

Dog tags are the most valuable thing that any child of a G.I. can own. They provide his name and his service number. With this information, Iris was able to obtain from the National Personnel Records Center her father's last known address. In addition, children of the post-war G.I.s have the advantage of knowing that if this is out of date, as he is probably still driving, the current address can be obtained through the state motor vehicle department. Through this system, but because of a similarity of initial, Iris first found an uncle. He was delighted and proceeded to try to persuade his brother to make contact with his German daughter. He refused. Embarassed, the uncle then took it upon himself to welcome Iris into the family.

In the hope that if she visited them she might either meet her father by chance or perhaps something could be arranged, Iris arrived in the United States in May 1998. By now she knew that she was her father's only daughter. He had two American sons. Would this be enough temptation for him to meet her?

Iris has the disadvantage of a poor command of English, so her comprehension of the letters she received may not be perfect. She has gradually worked out that since the death of his mother, her father has cut all ties with his family. He no longer lives in the same neighborhood. When she arrived, his family tried to make up for the situation with lots of interest and love. She met all her aunts, uncles, and cousins but not, as she had hoped, her father. She still refuses to give up and is convinced that one day, he will change his mind.

Someone else who has been accepted by everyone in the family but her father is Lesley G. of Australia, who feels that he rejected her at birth. At the age of 35, Lesley learned from her mother that her father was an American serviceman: "they had spent a wonderful year together until she discovered that she was pregnant. It seemed that marriage was not on his mind, he offered her money for an abortion." Lesley had been legally adopted by her stepfather with whom she had a good relationship. Therefore, loyalty bound her to him until his death.

Her search was initially based on hearsay: "I had no paperwork at all to prove he was an American; his name does not appear on my original birth certificate." Added to this, her father's name was quite a common one. Though she knew where he came from, international telephone inquiries did not have him listed. She decided to go to his hometown and ask around, convinced that someone would know him from youth. There she discovered that he had died in Florida, but she was able to obtain the name of a half-brother:

> He did not want to see me, but he did give me a phone number of an aunt in Minnesota and an uncle in San Diego. I rang the aunt, she didn't want to know either. The uncle in San Diego

was very upset that his brother had never mentioned a child in England [which was where Lesley was conceived]. He did give me a great deal of information which included the fact that my father had children by an English wife, *one of whom is only six weeks older than me.*

It would appear that this British wife had been deserted not long after she arrived in the States to join her husband, and the children of this marriage had ended up being raised by a step-father. With only sketchy details of where they might be, other than in the same state, Lesley tried directory inquiries but drew a blank. Not willing to return to Australia before she achieved something from the visit, Lesley took her story, slightly dramatized, she confesses, to the town police. A couple of investigative calls later, she had a phone number:

The phone was answered by my half-brother's daughter. I didn't say who I was but she gave me his mobile number, so he got the news that he had a sister while driving down the Interstate behind the wheel of a truck loaded with steel. He took it very well and we talked for a while. He was on his way to Chicago but we met the next morning at a truck stop. His wife and daughter and another brother also came to vet me, I think. This was also the first time that I saw a photo of my father. It was very emotional. We went to his house and my third brother arrived. We spent the day swapping stories about our upbringing. We have common experiences in that we have all been rejected to a certain extent by our father. I would have liked to see him and ask for an explanation for his actions. I would have liked him to know that despite him leaving my mother in dire circumstances [her parents threw her out] we managed very well without him.

In spite of this bitterness, Lesley still has a sense of grief and feels that to bring her search to a conclusion, she must visit her father's grave in Florida next time she is in the States.

The condemnation of the family and the refusal to offer a pregnant daughter any help may now seem archaic, but this was quite a common practice up to the late 1950s. One could even speculate that this fear kept a large number of young women from taking chances. There was no easy way out of the dilemna of unmarried pregnancy; sympathy and help were in short supply. There were some mother-and-baby homes run by charities or the Salvation Army. They were probably of greater benefit to wartime women in uniform who were usually a long way from home. An illegitimate pregnancy could be hidden by either allowing the home to arrange an adoption or set up the child with foster parents until the mother could readjust her life. There was always the hope of help from the father or the chance the mother might persuade her parents to accept the situation. Inevitably though, if this took too long, the child was confused.

Bill de Quick, a printer now living in Cambridge with a lot of community involvement, represents the many children of G.I.s who grew up in a children's home. There were many such establishments in the U.K. that have since come under the umbrella of The Children's Society. They, like other charitable organizations, have changed their operative style. Children in need of care are no longer kept in homes unless they have educative or long-term problems. The plan is to place them in a family atmosphere either by fostering or adoption. In conjunction with this, they operate a post-adoption and "in care" project with counseling and advice.

As a child, Bill had been told that both his parents were dead (which I suspect was a kinder explanation than to reveal to a child that it had been, in many cases, deserted). This he accepted until, as a teenager, an act of carelessness on the part of a staff member at a clinic where he was waiting for an inoculation gave him a new perception of himself. He was left in possession of his records, which curiosity prompted him to open. There he discovered that he was not an orphan; an address was listed for his natural mother. Fortunately, instead of causing shock, Bill saw it as fortuitous. He memorized her address. Though there was a possibility that this was out of date, he took the chance of sending her a Christmas card. To his delight, she responded and agreed to meet him.

From her, he learned the truth of his background. She had been married at the time of his birth and had been forced into the choice of husband or child. The embarrassment of deserting him is possibly why it took several meetings between them before she revealed any details of his father; he had been a bugler in the last African-American regiment to leave Tavistock, Devon. This finally explained Bill's coffee-colored skin.

It is worth adding at this point that color was not a problem with the citizens of the U.K. at that time. One could say that the offspring of these mixed-race liaisons have benefited by being left behind. Those born to wartime G.I.s from the South would have experienced the difficulties of a segregated life. In the U.K. they were rarely treated differently, and the majority, like Bill, have white partners.

For him, the fact of a missing father did not assume undue importance because, having been raised as an orphan, Bill had never known a father figure. In spite of his doubts that with a last name of Brown, he could be found, Bill gave in to his mother and had a try. With the clues he had and his father's unusual middle name, the Personnel Center in St. Louis was able to locate the G.I.'s file.

Bill was notified that his father had died in 1990 and left a family in Salt Lake City, Utah. Within four months he had found them and was made very welcome. It seems that they had always known about him. This new family is very different from his own, but he says, "there is a closeness and bonding which I want to foster."

Diane S. of Berkshire was left with foster parents until she was 7. When her mother married and had another child, on the pretext that she would make an admirable companion, Diane was adopted by her mother and her husband. From then on, the mother lived under a veil of secrecy and denial, which was bound to affect her first-born daughter.

Diane did not settle well in her new surroundings and eventually ran away from home when she was 11. She missed her foster parents. She was brought back to her mother and eventually sent to a boarding school.

It would be some time before Diane would learn the reasons for her disruptive background or discover that her father had been an airman at the U.S. base in Alconbury. When she finally learned his name, it proved to be a common one, though she was told that he had been at pains to point out that it ended with an "e."

The U.S. base in the U.K. where he had served continued to be used many years after the end of World War II so that Diane was able to arrange to examine the microfiche listing the men who had served there. There were several with her father's name, so she appointed a private investigator in the United States to follow through. This is a policy TRACE discourages. Experience has shown that such long-distance investigations are rarely successful. There are preferable avenues of research that can be pursued from the U.K. But Diane was not yet a member of TRACE.

In 1979 Diane applied to the National Personnel Records Center for information on her father, but this was before the court ruling that allowed certain information to be disclosed, and she therefore had no success. Some time later, she saw that there was to be a U.K. convention of U.S. private investigators in a nearby hotel, and thought a personal approach might work better, but the investigator she appointed made little headway. Her next attempt was through the locator column of the *Air Force Times*. That brought some replies, but none of them were positive enough to pursue. By now, though, she had acquired the number of her father's bomber group, which led her to the appropriate Veterans Administration. Some of these have proved helpful to people in the past; this particular one only suggested that she approach the "Find People Fast" locator service. From that she received a list of names and began to phone them: "all spoke quite freely, except one. He said that he had a problem and had to go and hung up."

Without making any accusations, experience tells us that men who hang up are more likely to have something to hide rather than being rude. This makes for a strong suspicion that the father has been found, especially since in this case, one of the investigators Diane retained had provided her with a printout of this particular person's driver's license, and certain details matched.

Diane's suspicions were aroused, but she chose to allow a few weeks before trying again: "this time, a woman answered and said that there was no one there by that name and hung up. I am scared to phone again in case they change their number or move." In case she did not have the right person, or possibly to confirm that she did, Diane decided to tackle her problem from a different angle that might not be seen as intrusive. She discovered that the editor of the Veterans of Foreign Wars (VFW) magazine had fifty subscribers with this name. He agreed that if she prepared a letter, he would mail it out to them. None replied.

By now, Diane had become a member of TRACE and attended the 1994 "Get Together" in Southampton, Hampshire. There, she was able to talk to Philip Grinton, one of our busiest helpers in the U.S. He sent her a very long list of servicemen with her father's name. It proved too daunting a task to follow them up, but the need to know something about her father or share some little part of him was still there.

In 1997, she saw an announcement that the Imperial War Museum was opening up at Duxford, once used as an U.S. Air Force base. (This building, dedicated to the history of flying, has since won a top architectural award.) She said, "I so desperately wanted to see a Flying Fortress B-17 [her father's plane]. I touched one! I just had to do this."

Diane has done no more searching, partly, I suspect, because though it is hard to concede, she knows that that earlier phone call has to be accepted as a rejection, and yet she is ready to excuse him for that: "there is no doubt that not having a father present in my life has been a devastating emptiness. I don't blame him, he didn't know. In my eyes he can do no wrong. I just want to say, 'Hello Dad' and look in his eyes. Time will tell perhaps."

Teresa M. of Northern Ireland knows quite a lot about her father. He was part of the early arrival of American troops in the U.K. During the romance with her mother, he gave her his identity bracelet, which some would have seen as a token of love and certainly, since it held his service number, indicates that he had nothing to hide.

> Apparently, my father was called back to the States before I was born. I was brought back from hospital to my grandparents home in Kilkeel Co. Down. My grandmother had 14 children of her own, and everyone of them are able to tell me something about my father. He visited the family home frequently. When I was old enough to understand, my grandmother told me who he was and pointed out that I had his hair colouring. We were both red-heads.

It appears that after his return to the United States Teresa's mother did keep in touch with her father for a while. Her grandmother told her that after she was born, her father wanted a lock of her hair, but she would not allow this for fear it would give him a claim, and he would want mother and child to come to him in America: "as my mother was only 16 or 17 years old, she was too young to go so far from home."

This tender age may also explain the reason for the G.I.'s sudden departure at the news of her pregnancy. He may have been unaware of the fact that he was consorting with an underage girl, or taken the chance. Once she was pregnant, it became a more serious matter, and he could face prosecution. It is possible that because of this he was allowed the escape of a transfer by his commanding officer.

Teresa's mother seems to have put the problem behind her, as she eventually married. Her child was left to be raised by Grandma and to this day the mother keeps up the pretense that they are "sisters." "I feel so deeply hurt, and terribly let down. I thought if I found my father and that he would want to know me and that would have made me feel a little bit of what a parent was like."

In mid-1998, Teresa was in New York visiting one of her children who was working there. She found her father in the phone book, but when she telephoned, he denied all knowledge of her. She does not wish to cause any disruption to his domestic life; there is always the possibility that there is a wife who has no knowledge of her husband's past. Therefore, Teresa has sent him a letter via the Veterans Administration in his state, and she hopes he will not reject it. She has written to tell him that he has a great big family in Ireland waiting to greet him; Teresa has eight children, and she enclosed a photograph of his five great-grandchildren carrying on the family tradition of red hair! Many months have passed; she has yet to get a response.

In July 1998, Jenny of Somerset wrote to say that after breaking down her list of names to four possibilities, three of whom were not the correct age, she wrote to the one she was positive was her father. He signed for the letter but did not reply:

I half expected it as his behaviour at the time I was born was hardly exemplary, but I made allowances because it was war-time and he was very young [only 22]. I do realise that it was an extraordinarily difficult and bewildering time for foreign youth sent overseas to fight at a time when people didn't travel like they do now. Also the philosophy of "live for today for to-morrow may never come" was understandable. Before I was born, my father signed a private paternity order at a local so-licitor [lawyer] agreeing to pay maintenance for me until the age of 16. They all went away just before D. Day and his friend wrote to my mother that my father was planning to forget about us once he got back to the States and that he was not a bad person, just weak.

My father did write and ask for a copy of my birth certificate and was supposed to have accelerated his transport home at the end of the war under the pretence that he was coming back to marry my mother and needed to sort out his affairs and bring back money. Rather a sorry tale!

Just over 2 years later on my third birthday, a letter arrived from my father's aunt. She wanted to know how I was and asked for photos and wanted to send a gift of clothing for me but my mother destroyed the letter. My grandmother managed to prevent her tearing up his photo. She said I might like it when I was older. She was right of course.

Jenny was subsequently brought up by her grandparents who legally adopted her when she was 5, but this was kept from her and became a terrible shock when discovered. Her search for her father began ten years ago:

The sense of loss I felt at that time has sadly never left me. Despite the outcome I will never regret looking for my father. For me it's been a sort of voyage of discovery and self discovery. Interesting to find out more about my paternal family and my own reaction to the way my father has behaved.

Susan P.'s mother was one of the wives who panicked at the foot of the gangplank as she was to board a war brides ship with her baby for a new life in the United States. She was never to join her husband; the marriage ended, and they went on with their lives.

This situation should not have had any bearing on Susan's relationship with her father, but there appears to have been little communication. She now has a debilitating illness and is in need of her full medical history to see what can be done.

When her father was found, in spite of the proof of the wedding certificate, photographs, and letters, he denied that he was that person. This is possibly because he did not reveal a first marriage when he embarked on the second. He has since died, and his children from that marriage are refusing to cooperate. Susan is now left in a precarious position; to be so close to what could be the most important part of her medical history and now not to be allowed access to that information seems extremely cruel. One can only hope that before it is too late, one of these relatives will exhibit some compassion on her behalf.

In 1976, Wayne's mother married his father, but when he left the Air Force base in Suffolk to return to the States, he did not arrange for his wife to follow him. No real explanation for this seems to have been offered their son, but when he was older, with knowledge of his father's home state, he obtained his current address through the motor vehicle department. The letter he wrote introducing himself received no reply, so he tried telephoning. One must accept that he had every legal right for this intrusion, but all he found was an answering machine. It did not seem appropriate for a "Hello Dad" message, so Wayne sought an alternative solution in case that answering machine, coupled with the fact that his father had not replied to his letter, was an act of rejection. He referred back to the phone book for other people with his same last name in the hope that they were relatives who might intercede on his behalf.

On the 14th September 1997, I received a phone call from my father's cousin, Frank. He told me that my father lived in the town but they did not see much of each other and that I had lots of family living in the state. We talked for some time and got on well, he told me he'd write more about the family.

A month went by and no letter arrived so I called and talked to another cousin. She told me that the rest of the family were very excited about me making contact. They seemed to care about me.

Wayne was heartened by the fact that the reason why his first cousin had not responded as promised had to do with a family illness, not neglect. Greatly encouraged, Wayne now felt that he was being accepted by these cousins, and there was a good chance that this would lead to his father. Sadly, another month went by with no communication: "I thought that the last thing I could do was send a Christmas card, some photos of my children and a copy of my birth certificate. I still had no reply and I don't feel I should telephone again. I don't want to be disappointed or to be too pushy. I have no idea if my father knows about me trying to make contact and how he feels about it."

Most TRACE members would tell Wayne to "go for it," but he would prefer a third party to intervene on his behalf. We have suggested that he ask the National Personnel Records Center to forward a letter, which they have done for people in a similar position. It would have to be signed for, and Wayne would know if his father actually received it. The other hope is that one of the originally enthusiastic members of his family will do something more for their English relative who wishes to be claimed.

What does one do when the details match, the ex-G.I. remembers one's mother, but he does not think that he is one's father? This has caused Alana H. of Bucks a problem.

> I spoke to his wife initially, they had married in 1949 and had no children. They have both been kind to me. He phoned back to say he remembered my mother but the timing seemed wrong for him to be my father. The records I then received from the National Personnel Office indicated that his service had ended in October 1945 which was definitely before I was conceived. All this seems to indicate that my mother definitely misinformed me. [She died two years ago] so I shall never know the truth.

What made the situation even more problematical was that this gentleman was keen to stay friendly; he sent Alana candy for her birthday and a photograph of him and his wife with an invitation to come and visit them: "it must have been quite a shock to both of them but I don't know what to do because I still don't know if he is my father and don't see how he can be if he wasn't in England at that time. It has left me feeling very confused."

The confusion continued because Alana accepted the invitation to visit the couple in America. There they who had been so open in their first encounters now seemed evasive, though the wife suggested a DNA test for her husband. He was not in very good health, so Alana was hesitant to follow this through. She had to accept that there was a possibility that her appearance in their lives and the fact that they were childless had promoted some wishful thinking: "so, I am left on an emotional rollercoaster. There was no real reason for my mother to have lied." This G.I. has since died, so Alana still has no real answers.

One can only conjecture on the reasons behind this situation, as in the other cases of rejection. There are certainly occasions when it is a protective instinct toward wife and American family or as simple perhaps as embarrassment or guilt of a youthful indiscretion. We have one case where outright denial in spite of match of date and base has been followed by invitations to visit. That has led to a continual correspondence and exchange of family photographs but never a parental declaration.

In spite of this, as will be seen, the percentage of acceptances vastly outnumbers the percentage of rejections. This makes the continued quest by these offspring of G.I.s all the more encouraging.

Chapter Seven

*A Thousand Butterflies in
My Belly*

> I just wanted you to know that 49 years after he left England for
> France and the South Pacific and told my mother that he would
> be back for me and her (I was then unborn) I finally found him.
> —Letter to TRACE, dated May 7, 1994

This will provide an antidote to the last chapter.

Michael James Lee, M.D., of a metals and alloys company in Sheffield, is now known in the United States as Jimmy Ward, Jr. He may
reside in the U.K. but, possibly due to his genes, he is the personi-
fication of the "American Dream" since he worked his way up
through a succession of jobs, from selling ice cream to delivering
bread, and is now a successful businessman living in a lovely home
in Yorkshire.

A business commitment in China delayed Michael's first meeting
with his father, but since then he has visited with him many times
and been engulfed by the family. Aided by the Kentucky Genealogical Society in the last part of his search, Michael was led to a tiny
town where a number of people knew his father, James Ward. He
visits him now so frequently, he has become part of the local scene.

In one of his recent letters to me he reflected on what would have
happened if his Dad had taken him to America as a baby, because
he has since met a cousin who was badly wounded in Viet Nam. He

knows that he, like all European, postwar G.I. babies, would have become part of the Viet Nam generation.

Michael may have grown up comfortable in the knowledge that he had an American father, but not everyone's reaction to such information is favorable. Kerry C. of Gloucester was angry. She proceeded to blame this missing father for everything that went wrong in her family's lives. His importance to her mother did not really register until, as she died, her last words were his name.

Among her mother's treasures were her lover's letters with his address. Kerry resolved to try to find him. She hoped that the fact that she was a child of the 1950s gave her the advantage of finding him alive. She was one of the earliest members of TRACE and was therefore advised to try the *Army Times* locator service, which was one of the best sources to use at that time. Within five weeks, he was found.

She discovered that while he had gone on with his life and married, he had always told his children that he had a daughter in England. Kerry came over to meet them all for Christmas in 1987. While there, she discovered the truth of her parents' relationship: "he told me that my mother had been the love of his life; even his ex-wife told me that my Dad should never have married her because he still loved my Mum. I only wish that I could have found my Dad while my mother was still alive."

Another person, who shall remain anonymous, who had been loading the blame on her father was to discover that it should have been directed at her mother. This woman from Albaching, Germany, did not at first realize that her mother had given in to her parents who did not want their daughter to go to the States. This disapproval at that time related as much to the fact that the United States seemed impossibly far away as to anti-Americanism.

Her father tried very hard to persuade her mother to join him in Kentucky; even his mother sent a welcoming letter, as she knew by now that she was the grandmother of a baby born there. It was to no avail; in Germany at that time, just as in the U.K., parents exerted strict control. The daughter stayed with them.

It would not be until 1992 that the daughter decided to try to find her father. The first attempt was through the Red Cross, but that did not prove successful, so more time elapsed. Then, through one of our members, Dorothea (who has given this chapter a name), contact was made with TRACE. We were now much more aware of all the electronic assistance available and the fact that there were places like the Amerika Haus in some of the larger towns in Germany who held the invaluable CD-ROMs of U.S. phone directories.

In September 1997, she obtained a telephone number of someone in the same town where her father lived: "this turned out to be my father's sister-in-law who told us that my father was married. She said that she would be willing to forward a letter to him. There was no reply. Repeated calls to this lady were either not connected, hung up or the person answering denied that she lived there."

It is very sad for her to have come so close and now after fifty years to be denied the opportunity to reach her father. One could only assume that after the initial enthusiasm to the call, this sister-in-law felt that she should not interfere and be responsible for disrupting a family member's life, or a family conference was needed. Whatever did happen, the outcome provided a success for the daughter. In April 1998, she had a call from her father, who was delighted to be found.

If the search for the G.I. father is initiated by the mother, it is often tinged with her curiosity as to what happened to the G.I. A frequent and useful excuse for a G.I.'s desertion had been that he was probably a casualty of the war. With the passing of time, as a sop to their conscience, they may encourage the child of this relationship to find out if he really did survive.

This was the approach taken by the mother of Diane Couchman of Northants: "she never mentioned my real Dad until about 3 years ago when she sort of hinted that she wanted me to find out if he was alive or dead. It just so happened that I saw in our local paper the address of Transatlantic Children's Enterprise. It was as if it was meant to be."

We redirected her from what would have been a false start by assuming from the APO number that her father was from New York. He was found in Pennsylvania, and she quickly learned that he had not willingly deserted her. Diane's father was a veteran with much military history. He had been an early arrival in the U.K. and from there was sent to North Africa in 1943, then to Italy in 1944 where he was injured. All his papers, which included her mother's address, were lost in transit. He was now relieved and delighted to be found, as were his children to meet her. She remarked, "I am sure that they accepted me because I have the family nose!"

There is a sad sideline to this story; Diane's British half-siblings are hurt by what she has done. This is an easy emotion for them to express from the security of knowing both their natural parents. They and others should try harder to understand that this need to find a missing link is not necessarily detrimental to any longstanding relationship but is a necessary piece of personal history.

Matching features play an important part in these searches and may overcome initial hesitation. This would take John Lancashire of Hertfordshire from despondency to joy. John had been adopted, but when he was quite small he found hidden letters indicating that his biological father was American and that he had an unusual last name. John remembers feeling glad that this made him "different," but youth and loyalty to his adoptive parents put any further action on hold for some time.

In 1997 he decided to join TRACE and was advised that while his father's last known address might be out of date, it did provide a good starting point. We also suggested that the most tactful approach would be via the Veterans Administration of that state. This did not bring him any response.

John started studying a map of the state and felt drawn to one town in particular. Following this hunch, he tried international telephone inquiries and was given the number of someone there with a similarly spelled last name. He said, "I waited a couple of days and then phoned and asked if he was John Hoogarhyde who was stationed in Bovingdon in 44/45." While this question produced an affirmative answer, when John continued the conversation his father said that he did not recall John's natural mother. John persevered with details from the letters that he had found in his youth, which included the fact that the G.I.'s parents were Dutch and that there was a brother Wesley. When this was confirmed, John knew that he had the right man, but by then the conversation had revealed that this gentleman had only recently been widowed so he was hesitant to continue. By now though, the man's curiosity had been aroused, and he wanted to know what the call was about:

> I said, "I think you are my father." There was a slight pause but he did not deny it but did not say he was either. He still could not recall my mother but because of what I knew about him, he said it could be right. Then, he said, "do you want to come out and see me?" He gave me his address and said I had given him something to think about and I could phone him again.

Convinced that he had the right man, John wrote a letter and enclosed some up-to-date photographs. Then, to make sure that they had arrived, he allowed an interval and then phoned. This time he was told by his father that he did not want to pursue this any further. He had seven children and did not want to upset them. Confusingly, he then added that he had come to Hemel Hempstead (the closest town to his wartime base) eight years ago and mentioned how much it had changed. John sensed a message in that statement but was not sure what it was, so, "I apologised to him and said that I had been kept in the dark for over 50 years and I just wanted to know who my father was and said goodbye."

When a disconsolate John, feeling very rejected, came back to us in November 1997, we advised patience. There is always the possibility of a problem where other siblings are concerned. One has to accept that the father's revealing of this piece of his past may not go down too well with the American children. They can become very territorial or question if this claim on the family may be for financial gain. We suggested that John keep the connection going, and with Christmas approaching, a festive card would be appropriate and leave room for a follow-up. This worked: "I had a reply before Christmas. He said that he did not know what to say to me and he still thinks that he is not my father but will give me the benefit of the doubt. He asked me to send a photo of my mother [John had by now located her] and one of me. I in turn asked him to send me some photos of himself."

To give John some peer-group, emotional support, we had by now also put him in touch with one of our other members, Norma Jean Clarke, who had overcome several obstacles to reach her father.

In the spring of 1998, I received a letter from John, which was a tumble of emotions. He had again used the excuse of making sure that his mail had arrived to get an update on the situation:

> I said if he did know my mother to come clean and admit it. I did get a reply and he was a bit annoyed the way I worded my letter. He said that he did know my mother but that did not mean he was my father, but he said that there was a strong resemblance between us when we were teenagers. So, he would leave it to me to decide. Enclosed were two photos of himself in 1946 and 1996.

In spite of what John saw as obvious facial similarities, he wrote back to say that he did not want him to be his father if it were not true, but he did add that he believed it was. This firmness on John's part is a good example of how to deal with a situation that has no real reason to falter. Why walk away from the obvious without making a stand?

For John, this proved successful; his father phoned back with an apology, which partially explained his hesitancy in making claim to him. It was born of defensive thinking, which is often evident if there was more than one boyfriend in the equation, as was the case with John's mother. There was, however, no denying that they were father and son after seeing the photographs. "my father said I should have got in touch with him thirty years ago. I said I would like to meet him and he said he is nearly ready for the boneyard so he can't come to England. I said I would go to him and he said I would be most welcome."

In July 1998, John reported back on that visit, which began with a renewal of uncertainty because, when he arrived at the airport, he could not see anyone that he recognized from the photographs. The simple explanation turned out to be that they showed no comparison in height:

> And then, this small guy walked up to me and I realised it was him. We shook hands and then drove the 70 miles to his hometown. On the way, he talked of his time in Hemel Hempstead and my mother and then he said that he was still not sure he was my father. This made the whole journey seem a waste of time. He left us at our motel and said he would phone next morning which he did. We then went to his house and talked some more. His youngest daughter came in and said she did not mind a bit about me being his son.

This, John would find, applied equally to his father's other children: "we saw each other every day and got much closer. On the Friday night, John, my wife his son David and I went to a bar and he introduced me as his son from England and this made me feel very proud."

On Sunday they went to dinner at another sister's house, and John was moved to tears when grace was said because they included thanks for the fact that he and his wife were now part of the family. His emotions went into overflow with the next surprise: "they knew it was our wedding anniversary and had arranged a celebration. When we went across the border to a restaurant in Canada, bells, horns and sirens rang and the barmaid said, 'please welcome John and Olwen from England on their 30th wedding, anniversary.' My father then said, 'tell them the whole story that I am your Dad.' "

John, who had so worried that when he went to America it would be a disaster, now says: "I could not have asked for anything better. I am so glad that I traced him."

The one thing that I request from all our members once they are reunited with their fathers or families is that they send me a photograph. The collection is beginning to cover half of my office wall.

John's showed that while he is head and shoulders taller than his father, the family connection is distinct—they both have the same nose!

John's closing comment on his reunion could be echoed by many others within the group: "I wish that I had done this 20 years ago." There is an even happier postscript to this story. In a letter to me dated October 1999, John reported on a second visit to his father. "When it came time to leave, Dad was crying. I put my arms around him and said, 'I am so glad you are my Dad.' He said, 'Thank you, John, for saying that.' "

Christopher Eborn was stunned when he went through family papers after his father died and for the first time discovered that he was not his parents' natural son. With the support of the Social Services Adoption Department, he learned that his natural father was a Sgt. Arthur Bobb, USAF, who had paid for his birth and maintenance for six months. The papers also revealed that his natural mother had tried hard to keep him, but it had proved too difficult. He said, "I was glad that I had found my history. This is no disrespect to the parents who had brought me up and who I will always see in this way."

Given this strong loyalty to his adoptive parents, Christopher was hesitant to proceed. It took three years for him to make up his mind. The first step in these cases of adoption is usually to find the natural mother who might be able to fill in extra details. The paperwork showed that she had been married and divorced. Whether it was because of his inner fear of rejection, part of British reticence, or the draw of the unknown in America, Christopher chose to try to find his American father.

TRACE always tries to put new members in touch with someone who is compatible to their case. For Christopher, it was Dot R., who has established certain connections that lead to men based at the USAF base at Ruislip, where Christopher's father had served. She also had access to the Internet and the advantage of knowing this unusual last name. There proved to be only six people listed with it. For some reason that Dot cannot explain, she decided to start with the bottom one and, to safeguard Christopher from rejection, made the initial phone call. She said, "his immediate response was, 'how is Christopher, what can you tell me about him?' this was followed by, 'tell Christopher he can write or phone me, whatever he wants to do.' "

With a large drink in hand for courage, Christopher chose to make a phone call. There was no answer. He tried again, confessing that at that moment, he thought his father had, to use an English expression, "done a runner." But he was to be third time lucky: "I went, 'Hi', he went, 'Hello'. I said, 'I don't know what to call you, father, Dad, Sir'; I was a quivering, shaking wreck."

Christopher quickly discovered how glad his father was to be found and that he had actually come over to England in the 1980s to try and find him by going through the telephone directories looking for someone with his old girlfriend's maiden name: "not knowing that I had been adopted, he would never have found me and yet, as he showed his daughter round his old Base, he did not know how close by I lived."

Christopher was to discover that he had three brothers and one sister, but only his father's eldest son knew about him. We have found that this is often the case; the ex-G.I. who is concerned about the child he left behind needs to "unload" on someone—either brother or son though, interestingly enough, rarely a daughter—except, as will be seen, in an obscure way. While the rest of the family were being told, he and his father exchanged telephone calls, letters, and photographs.

Before long, the father wanted to know when Christopher could come over and visit them. When he explained that it was a question of saving up for the fare, his father offered to pay. He declined. Then, an unexpected phone call from one of his brothers convinced him to allow their father the pleasure of sending those tickets.

The plan was for Christopher and his wife to fly in to Dulles Airport in Washington, D.C., close to where his sister lived. As the plane landed, he became overwhelmed with emotion:

> I said to my wife, I don't think I can walk off. Even at this stage, I was scared stiff. Was this the right thing I'm doing, are they going to like me, am I going to like the rest of the family. As I walked through, my sister came running over, we hugged and then, I turned, and there was this man of 59 [Christopher is a 1950s baby]. We looked at each other, eyes watery. I had already been warned by one of my brothers that Dad was not a toucher, it would be shake hands.
> "Pleased to meet you, Sir."
> "Pleased to meet you, Christopher."
> In ten seconds, with those few words, I knew that I had made the right decision.

They spent the first few days in the Washington area with Christopher's sister, much of the time taken up with questions and answers. Then it was a four-hour drive to where the rest of the family lived and arrival at a house decorated with welcome signs and balloons: "everything was right and it kept getting better. They all wanted a piece of me. We all look alike, Mike the second youngest is me, 10 years ago, so obviously, my father's genes were the strongest!"

Christopher became absorbed in all aspects of Americana. This included time spent in his father's cabin in the woods, deer spotting, hunting, and preparing the kill. In the privacy of that cabin, Christopher and his father had the opportunity for a heart-to-heart talk: "my father said words that mean a million pounds to me. 'If your father [adoptive] is still alive, I'd like to shake his hand and say thank you for bringing you up and looking after you' and we agreed as a mark of respect to my adoptive father, we would stay on first name basis."

By now, the eldest American brother knew that Christopher had written a book on the Rolling Stones and that, in fact, some of the memorabilia he had that related to them was on exhibit at the Rock and Roll Hall of Fame in Cleveland. They all wanted to see it. Christopher was astonished to learn that they would contemplate a seven-hour drive to do so: "we hired a small limo and I arranged with the Curator of the Museum to give us a VIP tour. This took us to exhibits marked: 'from the Chris Eborn Collection.' "

One can imagine how proud they were of their reception. However, it later developed that family influence worked both ways. The last leg of their journey was again spent in Washington, D.C., so that Christopher and his wife could do some sightseeing. His sister there had her own set of "connections" and was able to arrange for them to have a private tour of the White House.

Recovering from this whirlwind visit to his family, as he boarded the plane back to England, Christopher mistakenly handed over his American Express card instead of the boarding pass. When the flight attendant learned the reason for the confusion, she was back a few moments later to insist that he and his wife were in the wrong seats. It developed that the crew had been so intrigued with his story that they wanted to make their own contribution to this special trip: "we were ushered into Club Class so we flew back in style which was an appropriate way to end the visit. I am really pleased I did it. I've got this great man in America who has—the only way of saying it is that he has replaced a great man who brought me up in England. I have been lucky twice."

There is a charming postscript to this story. The Rolling Stones were due in concert in Philadelphia, so Christopher's sister phoned to see if he was coming over for it. To please her, he did and also arranged for them to have VIP tickets and a backstage introduction. He reports that: "she was somewhat dumbstruck!"

Diana Rosswinkel of Siershahn, Germany, is a 1960s baby who was 10 when she found her adoption papers. At that age the significance of the discovery is having a secret to hold silently over the family. It was not until she was older that taking this information any further became important. From the *Jugendampt*, she was able to obtain the name of her father and what appeared at first to be his service number. This proved incomplete, which is another example of carelessness on the part of the authorities, like not ensuring that the father's name is spelled correctly, that leads to later problems. However, one must accept, of course, that in wartime conditions or the adjustment to peace such records were taken down in a hurry and not always given in detail.

Diana chose at that stage to get on with her life, but after the failure of her marriage decided to make a concerted effort to find her roots. This led to the discovery that her mother had given up another child for adoption who, by coincidence, had called at the *Jugendampt* just four weeks earlier looking for her records.

In some excitement, Diana contacted this half-sister, but they did not find that they had enough in common to establish a satisfactory relationship, so the need was even greater to find her father and hope that would be successful. In 1994, she saw some information about TRACE on German television. At this stage, if they were lacking much detail and, for instance, only had the name of the father's home state, we were suggesting that they pick a few towns at random and try them out through international directory inquiry.

This did not provide a solution for Diana, but the motor vehicle department did provide an update of her father's address. We advised her to write to him and include her telephone number:

> I was frightened to intervene in his family life, they might not know about me and it is not easy to write to someone you know, only from the address and date of birth, so I wrote formally addressing him as Mr Christopher and then explained enough for him to recognise who I was, and added that there were no financial reasons for the letter and included photographs of me and my child. But, I still hesitated before I posted this.

Diane need not have worried; a week later her phone rang—it was her father. They talked for an hour, and he kept repeating how happy he was to be found. He explained that all his family knew that he had a child in Germany, and he had tried several times to find her. As is often the case, unless the natural father knows who the adoptive family are (and this is highly unlikely), finding the child they have left behind is an impossible task.

Diana's father invited her to come over to the States, but because probably she preferred the security of her home ground for this first meeting, she asked him to come to Germany with his wife. Six weeks and many telephone calls later, Diana met them at Frankfurt Airport: "when I saw him, I had the feeling that I had known him all my life."

She has since been over to the States and has been happily absorbed into a large, loving, warm family. This compensates somewhat for the fact that she later discovered that her natural mother had married a G.I. and gone to live in the States. Their reunion did not have the same happy ending, which may indicate that Diana has a greater proportion of her father's American genes!

During the fighting that followed the invasion of France, Elbert Bridges of South Carolina was taken prisoner of war at St. Lo. Because of the shortage of able-bodied men, he had the good fortune to be sent to work on a German farm instead of going to a prisoner-of-war camp. There, he romanced the farmer's daughter, and once they knew a child was on the way they discussed names. If it was a girl, she would be named for his sister Doris. However, at the end of the war, when the G.I. was repatriated, a confusing letter arrived from Germany, which indicated that his lady love had married someone else, so he went on with his life.

In fact, Dorothea's mother did not marry, and the child learned about her American father when she was 6 years old. Such truths do not register with small children who are more interested in the present, so it was some time before she took any action. When she began to wonder about her father, she started a search of secret places, which led to a tin box tucked in the sewing machine drawer. Because of his prisoner-of-war status, the information she found was minimal but all she needed—his field number, name, date of birth, and home state, plus a homemade ring that became her greatest treasure: "one of my mother's friends told me that my father was a handsome young man and I often said to my mother, 'I'll look for him when I have enough money.' "

In the 1950s, as they listened to the news of the war in Korea on the radio, Dorothea was concerned that this might affect her American father. Her mother's response was obviously designed to give her daughter pride in her American heritage. She agreed that this was possible because Americans are always there to fight for others in the world.

Dorothea ended up waiting until her mother died before starting her search. She was motivated by the anniversary of the end of the war in Europe: "on the night of 8/9 May [1995], I sat down and wrote my own personal record with a request to TRACE to help me look for my father."

This was translated by Inge Gurr, and we discussed the reply, which would be to advise Dorothea to start with the motor vehicle department as she had her father's last known state. This seemed more advisable than a direct approach through telephone inquiries because Dorothea was anxious not to intrude on her father's life. At this stage she also knew very little English and worried that this was going to cause a communication problem when she found her father.

After four weeks, she received his up-to-date address, and with the help of a friend, she composed a letter in English. With a strong inner feeling that he would want her, she counted off the days as she waited for a reply. Time began to stretch beyond her patience, and she phoned Inge for advice. She was reassured that experience has proven it takes a father time to come to terms with such unexpected news. We suggested she stay calm.

On December 12, Dorothea received a Christmas card and a letter that said her father was the happiest man in the world: "I thought to lose the ground under my feet and I have had 1000 butterflies in my belly. This feeling is not really to describe and no one can feel and understand the same without it was one in the same situation."

Dorothea had so much to say to her father that she took along her friend as translator for this first visit. The ring that was a souvenir of her parents' romance was the most important item of her luggage. It was ceremoniously handed over to her father who told her that he had originally lost it working in the farm stables.

Elbert Bridges, a widower with no children, became on receipt of that first letter a father and grandfather. His daughter is now learning English. To him should go the last words since he has gone from being alone to becoming a member of a large family. On one occasion when Dorothea visited and he was not very well, he had the newly found pleasure of the tender care of a loving daughter:

> Since Dorothea's first letter, we have become a close family. She has visited me here in South Carolina and presented me with three grandchildren, all grown up and as of this letter, I have two gt. grandchildren. I have made two trips to Germany and visited with family and old friends [on the farm that Dorothea has inherited from her mother].
>
> God Bless, keep up the good work and once again, Thanks! Thanks! Thanks!

Chapter Eight

"Helping Hands"

> I have been given your address by the American Embassy. I am
> the surviving daughter of Corporal William G. Chambless U.S.
> Army 18040 who was killed in action in Belgium in 1944. My
> mother failed to follow up the opportunity to contact his family
> in USA and so I have never really known anything more about
> him than his name.
>
> —Letter dated November 10, 1988,
> from Sue Fenton in search of some background
> on the American half of her family

William G. Chambless was a small-town boy from Alabama whose
first ride on a train was to his Army camp. He came to the U.K. to
begin training on Salisbury Plain in Wiltshire for the invasion of
France. On an off-duty visit to the American Red Cross Club, he met
and fell in love with a young woman who was studying at a nearby
teacher training college. He wrote home to tell his family that he
hoped to marry his British sweetheart. This was never to be, but
before he left for the forthcoming battle in Europe, he discovered
that he was to be a father. Aware of the dangers ahead of him, he
made sure that his future child would have the support of an Army
pension if he did not survive.

Sue Fenton thought that the details on the pension paperwork
would enable her to find her American family. Unfortunately, the
number on that paperwork had not been transposed correctly, and

therefore it did not match the files with the G.I.'s service number. To add to the problem, she accepted from her mother that the middle initial of her father's name stood for George. With this incorrect and minimal information, and the fact that electronic tracing aids were in their infancy, it appeared that she was reaching a dead end.

Some years later, I did an interview on the CNN International Hour in which I discussed the difficulties of finding G.I. fathers and family, and Sue's impasse was broken. Among the many people who phoned or wrote in from the States offering to help was "Bud" Shapard, living at that time in West Virginia. His career background gave him the additional expertise in finding people that he was now willing to share. After a lengthy investigation, he came up with someone he felt was a match to Sue's father. She was not sure that she agreed: "Bud said that the only person who fitted the bill had a middle name of 'Gaines' whereas I was sure that it was George—the truth is probably that Mum didn't even know what his middle name was and invented George—who knows?"

What we do know is that the British of that time were not used to unusual first names any more than the foreign-sounding last names that so many of the American troops carried. Also, there is a tendency for people to suffer a fluttering fear of rejection when they get this close to the truth. Invariably, last-minute reasons arise as to whether they might have the wrong person.

Bud Shapard was convinced enough he was correct that he was determined to get enough confirmation to satisfy Sue. This took time. A letter from Sue dated February 17, 1997, stated:

> Truly wonderful news. Just before Christmas Bud Shapard phoned to say that he had made contact with my father's half-brother. Within hours my uncle was on the phone to me and the next day, I had a call from an aunt as well. And, all of a sudden, I had a family. Since then we have all been busy catching up, letters with photos, phone calls. . . . at last I have a recognizable picture of my father. . . . I never thought the journey would be such an emotional one when I started just over 9 years ago, nor that I should be so lucky as to have such delightful relations. [It was obviously unfinished business for them too.] We all hope to meet as soon as we can afford the trip, hopefully with Mum who would dearly love to visit my father's grave.

One of the most poignant parts of this story relates to how this family in the States came to terms with the G.I.'s death. They decided that, as he had fallen in love with a British girl, he had faked his death in order to live there in England with her and the child. Sadly, in the 1950s reality set in when they had him brought back from Europe to be buried at home in Alabama.

Bud Shapard had made it clear to me from the start that he would only work solo with anyone who wanted his help because duplication of effort is time destroying. He was even willing to write the appropriate letters needed to accompany the initial investigation. Commendation for these methods is offered by Sue: "I have to say I like the way Bud works, he has been so helpful, writing letters for me to sign and doing it all with a personal touch that makes me hope that one day we will meet." This has yet to happen, but a member of her father's family has been over to meet Sue. Together they retraced the places where he had spent time on British soil. Then, when in 1998, the film *Saving Private Ryan* was issued in the U.K., Sue determinedly suffered through the battle sequences to try to share some of her father's last experiences.

Not everyone is willing to accept Bud's singular method of research or exercise the patience that is required. As has been seen, children of G.I.s have a desperate need that can only be fed by the feeling that they are "doing something." As time goes by, they may recognize that they need more guidance.

Carole O., a nurse living in Somerset, approached us in 1990 knowing only her father's name and home state. She pursued a series of suggestions that we made, none of which resulted in any success until 1995, by which time we had access to our most reliable source of information, CD-ROM telephone directories that were being installed in many British reference libraries.

In this manner she found two people with her father's name listed in Virginia. This led to the discovery that her father was dead: "I felt I had lost someone I had known—had to go through a form of bereavement ceremony to say 'goodbye' but this strengthened my desire to know my family and history."

The state of Virginia is close by Bud Shapard's home, and he took over. He found a minister of the church in her father's home area who was willing to act as intermediary with the family; they had known nothing about the child in Europe, but that did not deter them from filling Carole in on the family history. She was to discover that she came from a long line of achievers:

After many weeks, I received a letter from a cousin of my father. He was very surprised to hear about me but also very pleased. My father was one of seven children. His father was a black minister for over 40 years and a pioneer in education. He

founded [a] high school which is in existence today. All his children excelled in various professions including my father who
was a school principal. Unfortunately, they are all deceased
and more tragically and unbelievably, none of them had any
children. This of course means that, *I am the only grandchild*
of my father's parents.

Carole has been showered with relatives but not the half-brothers
or sisters that she had hoped for and with whom she could share
some memories of her father. Her biggest bonus is the elderly cousin
who made the initial contact; he was brought up in the same area
as her father and will be able to fill her in on his formative years. He
sent her a family tree and she has since met many relatives.

While I try hard not to play favorites, William Stroobants in Belgium will always be special to me. He first approached TRACE in
1992 searching for his father whom he had known about since he
was 18. This G.I. proved to be the classic illustration of a Jewish
boy from Brooklyn whose studies to become a lawyer had been interrupted by World War II. By 1992, we had realized that most men
fitting this description were unlikely to still be living in Brooklyn,
but this had to be used as a starting point because by now William
had been notified by the National Personnel Records Center that his
father's files had not survived the St. Louis fire. Other logical lines
of inquiry like the Veterans' Administration office in New York could
not help without additional data, which William did not have. Nor
did he yet know that he had the incorrect spelling of his father's
name. He tried the Jewish Genealogical Society and the mayor of
New York whose responses also proved negative.

It is not until someone has exhausted all the possibilities attached
to their clues that we suggest bringing in a U.S. helper, and now
seemed the time to appeal to Bud Shapard. He had the expertise
and more access to U.S. local telephone directories than William
had in Belgium. He was able to contact five families with the G.I.'s
name in New York City, but they were all either suspicious or reluctant to give out much information.

Bud suggested to William that it might be worthwhile to contact
the *Daily Forward*, a newspaper in New York City with a Jewish
circulation that has a column for missing relatives. The ad was
picked up by Rene Steinig in Dix Hills, New York who is a genealo-
gist. She said, "I am fascinated and challenged by such inquiries
and often assist people for no fee if I can help for a good purpose."

The important element called "luck" had entered the equation.
The woman went on to explain that she had consulted her national

computer database and come up with two possibilities, but before taking them any further, she had some concern. If he was a son looking for a father, what were his reasons? She emphasized everything that TRACE always does—that consideration must be made for the shock of this unexpected news and what it could do to a wife and children who knew nothing about this extra child.

William phoned me for advice on how to proceed, and I suggested that, as was our custom, he write a letter that should be prefaced with an apology for intruding in case he had the wrong man. By following this suggestion, William received an answer very quickly: "he wrote that he was glad I had found him. He said he was my father [the confirming clue was the name of William's mother] and that the fact that his parents did not want him to marry a Gentile was the reason he never told his wife or children."

The day the letter arrived, the ex-G.I. did tell his wife. He delayed telling his children until it was closer to the time when William was due to visit them all in California. He need not have worried; they welcomed him into the family. Without wishing to denigrate this situation, we have found that this generosity of spirit towards a new member coming into the family is always easier when the child is part of the father's premarital past.

What was to follow was even more admirable. This would be the first of three meetings between father and European son. One was a trip that the G.I. and his wife made to Belgium to meet the rest of William's family and pay a visit to the memorial of the Battle of Bastogne in which he had been a participant. The second was a trip for William to the States.

Sadly, the G.I. died on January 5, 1998, but this did not cut off William's link with his American family. They notified him of what had happened, and he took a night flight to California. He was met by his brother Eric and drawn into the funeral proceedings: "the service was held on Tuesday afternoon. I was introduced to everybody as Murray's son from Belgium. I took part in all the Jewish ceremonies praying every night and a service in the Synagogue on Friday." In the obituary, he was placed first as the eldest child, and his children were listed alongside their American cousins. The family gave William his father's bar mitzvah ring, which he wears with pride. I must intrude to make a personal comment here. As a Jewish person, I am always concerned when faced with this kind of case because we have had some very negative responses from families when there are people looking for Jewish fathers. This one made me very proud.

Wilfried Lebe from Riedering, Germany, was born in 1948 and was 8 when he found a hidden photograph of an American soldier. He confronted his mother, who admitted that this was his father, but she did not offer a name or home state until he was 10. This was still not an age for a boy to be very concerned to start a search.

The following year, prior to emigrating to the States, an aunt, trying to be helpful (or possibly to put him off any thought of looking for his father), told Wilfried that the G.I. had been killed in Korea. He was still too young to see much significance in that news. It would not be until 1993 after the death of his stepfather that he would decide to try to find out more about his natural father.

He did not realize the great advantage of the name and state until he contacted TRACE. The motor vehicle department in Pennsylvania gave him addresses for three men with the same name as his father and telephone numbers for two of them: "the first had never been in the Army, was very rude and insisted that he had never been in Germany. The second was kind and responsive but had only served in Japan. The third was unlisted."

People with unlisted telephone numbers are the most difficult to reach. They do not appear on the CD-ROMs of U.S. phone directories, which are our greatest access to information. We therefore put Wilfried in touch with Virginia Holden, who has already been mentioned in an earlier chapter. As a resident of the state of Pennsylvania she obtained the phone number by other means. Wilfried said, "my father who has a wife Peg was very friendly. He has a son called Larry and the amazing coincidence is that we three men are all auto mechanics."

The next step was to meet them all, but he was very concerned when his plane suffered a five-hour delay. In spite of that, the family were still at the airport waiting to welcome him, and great celebrations were planned: "father has a summer place and they put on a special firework display in my honour and then, he rented a hall in Altoona for a family reunion which brought in 100 people."

Virginia Holden had a hand in another such big reunion. John Korchak from Ipswich was the son of a marriage that had broken up, but his mother would not discuss the circumstances that led to it. His grandmother told him when he was 10 that his mother was a G.I. bride who had had second thoughts at the last minute and refused to go to the States. Again, he was too young to pry into any further detail, nor did he pursue the subject during his mother's lifetime: "in my 20s and 30s, I was so busy with my own family that I rarely gave the subject much thought. When my mother died, it was my son who started me on the search. He wanted to know more about his family background. My wife found a copy of your book in the local library."

John had his father's hometown, which was in Pennsylvania, and once he sent this to Virginia Holden, she found the family very quickly. Unfortunately, John's father had died ten years previously:

> This came as a bitter disappointment but there were many family members still alive. Within weeks they had sent me albums of photos of my father and the rest of them. We wrote to each other many times over the following months. I well remember Christmas Day 1994 when I received a phone call from my father's one remaining brother and his wife. I was in tears. We were invited over and stayed three weeks. We had a terrific time and stayed with various members of the family and were treated royally. We met Virginia Holden and her husband at the family reunion which was a very moving day and was reported in the local press. I think that this is one of the most positive things I have done in my life; in hindsight, I wish I had acted earlier in order to meet my father. TRACE has given me a whole new family. I might never have met them if it had not been for your contacts.

I concur about the contacts; we owe a debt to several people in the States who have willingly given their time and often their money (in spite of the fact we advise that international response coupons always be included in the mail, the postal costs, which can be sizable, are not always reimbursed).

Another volunteer came via my first book, *Sentimental Journey,* which she found in the Cleveland library. As someone who had worked with the U.S. Air Force in Melchbourne, England, Joan Peterson found it very nostalgic and wrote to me via the publisher. Never one to miss an opportunity for extra help, I quickly enlisted her to the cause of G.I.s' children in Europe. Joan is an ex-Londoner who started with the advantage of the mass of reference material available in the Cleveland, Ohio, library and the patience to thread flimsy clues together until they build many a reunion. Her capacity for searching has now been greatly enlarged by the advent of the Internet with which she is now fully acquainted. This has brought some long-term situations to a speedier conclusion. However, the following illustrations of some of her work were mostly accomplished by the more old fashioned, page-turning method of research.

TRACE was approached by a woman searching on behalf of her son. The G.I. who was the woman's boyfriend had signed an affidavit of responsibility before he left the U.K. in 1945. We usually avoid this kind of "old girlfriend" scenario. It belongs in the past, and we do not want TRACE to gain a reputation for aiding and abetting such situations. However, there was something about this particular appeal that eliminated either idle curiosity or worse—the danger of vengeance, which we work hard to avoid. Joan and I agreed that this request had the air of something special.

The woman had not told her son about his G.I. father until he was grown. His initial reaction had been shock and dismay; he was not particularly impressed by Americans. It was obvious that, given these circumstances, his mother wanted to remedy this.

Joan found the veteran, who was delighted by the news. He was, by now, living alone and not in the best of health, so travel back to the U.K. to visit her and their son was out of the question. For the next three years, "Mom and Pop" had a Sunday night conversational date. The son gradually recognized the importance of those phone calls to the quality of his mother's life. He accepted that their reunion would be even more enhanced if he and his father actually met. A visit was arranged.

The devotion between these two wartime lovers was even more apparent to the son while he was in the States, and he telephoned Joan Peterson and told her that his one wish now was to reunite his parents. This was never able to happen; the G.I. died before it could be arranged.

His American daughter was by then also aware of this enduring love story, and in recognition of the strength of the couple's feelings for each other, she sent her father's ashes to England. The English woman made a special journey to scatter them over their wartime trysting place. She said, "there is still that feeling of something missing on a Sunday evening. Sunday is a day I spend entirely on my own—very rarely speak to anyone and 8 PM was something to brighten the day and look forward to. However, I had seven years of talking to him and the occasional letter. I believe I must be one of the luckier ones."

Can one call this a happy ending? Very few broken romances of that period reach such a surreal conclusion. Much depends on the circumstances, and, sadly, bitterness seems to overcome the memory of other emotions involved. It was fear of the unknown country and the man's background, as well as parental responsibilities, that stopped many a British girl, pregnant or not, from accepting the G.I.'s offer of marriage.

Margaret's mother is one of the women who refused. In spite of this, on his return to the States, the G.I. sent money for the baby on a regular basis until she told him not to communicate further. She did not tell her daughter anything about her American father until she was grown.

Margaret began her search for him in 1992 by contacting Joan. She had the advantage of knowing his unusual name, his home town, and state. In this case it did not prove much help, but that there were not many people with this name listed in the telephone directories was favorable. They provided a starting point and cut down on the number of letters of inquiry, which in some cases run into hundreds. The object of all of them is the hope that one will lead to at least a relative of the father.

Joan had done the groundwork; it was now up to Margaret to follow through with an explanation of her interest in this family name. She received a reply from someone who was delighted to claim her as an uncle. He told her that his brother had carried a photograph of Margaret's mother in his wallet but had not revealed that there was a child. He said that as the Englishwoman had turned him down he would never marry and had led a solitary life, spending much of the time in his cabin by a lake. He had died in 1987.

The following year, Margaret, an attractive, well-dressed blonde who is a successful businesswoman, came over to meet two elderly uncles. They were enchanted with her. Since then, they have been over to England to meet family and friends, but the woman who broke their brother's heart will not receive them.

The American family are trying to persuade Margaret to settle in the States, but not only does she have her business commitments but her mother is now ailing and she will not leave her.

In contrast to the broken-hearted G.I. who felt he had only one love in his life is the one who was married and the father of three children when he arrived. The result of his romance while in the U.K. left a young woman with a child. She later married a man who turned out to be a very unkind stepfather. We have found that too many Englishmen who condescended to marry what they saw as "spoiled goods" took out their jealousy of the G.I. who went before them in verbal or physical abuse on the child.

Often, as in this case, it accelerates the child's need to find his or her American father. In this instance, the G.I. was by now divorced from the wife to whom he had been unfaithful, and he had married again. He was delighted with his pretty daughter and two small grandchildren in England. There were phone calls, letters, and photographs exchanged, but the second wife did not prove to be pleased. She, unlike others met in these pages who either feel they have nothing to fear or are happy for their husbands, was not as tolerant.

She accused his English child of being a fortune hunter and insisted on blood tests. Even this proof of paternity did not appear to satisfy her. The reunion between father and daughter began to suffer damage. It frosted the visit to America and began to impinge on the telephone calls. It became an untenable situation, and she wrote one last letter to her father: "I told him that I could not handle the wife. He wished me well but does not contact me anymore. No matter the result, I'm glad that I found him, he was a lovely man. I can close a passage of my life that was eating away at me."

We, of course, have to accept that we cannot achieve all happy endings! In spite of this, Joan, who shares the disappointment, would like to make one more comment on this work in which she has become so happily involved: "A G.I. stationed in Northern Ireland in 1943 fathered a daughter. His kin were located and conveyed the sad news that he had died in a car accident in the mid '80s. He will never know that his granddaughter became Champion Irish Dancer five years in a row."

Someone else who has to deal with the frustrations of unhappy endings is Mickey Olsen, a G.I. bride from Nottingham, who first went to Illinois but is now retired with her husband in Florida. She is one of our volunteers that I have since met while on a research trip there. Mickey spotted the tail end of my CNN International Hour interview and wrote to me via the network with an offer of help.

I was curious to know what had promoted her interest in TRACE and discovered that her sensitivity to missing fathers came from the fact her British father had deserted her mother before she was born. As she was from Nottingham, I assumed that she had married a man in the 82nd Airborne who were stationed there. She was therefore sent queries from people looking for fathers who had been in the 82nd because our practice is to match up wherever possible.

Then, I learned that Mickey's husband had been in the U.S. Air Force, and they had met when he was on leave looking over the ancient Nottingham castle. In spite of my mistake, she had already dealt with one 82nd Airborne search, which left her infuriated. This particular father refuses to accept or deny his paternity. In spite of that he and his wife communicate with his "daughter" and have invited her into their home. The only thing missing is the use of that magic word, "Dad." At least one of her other "82nd" tasks proved more rewarding.

Janet M.'s father was stationed in Leicestershire, which also hosted the 82nd prior to the invasion of France. The men there were stationed among British civilians, many of whom made them welcome in their homes. At that time, Janet's mother was already separated from her British husband, but when the romance culminated in a child, it was registered in the mother's married name. When the war was over, this lady was encouraged by her parent to reconcile with her husband. He adopted the baby. Janet was one of the more fortunate children in such a position; she was not made to suffer for what her mother had done, though there were stipulations to the agreement: "I always had a lot of respect from and for my mother but there was much shame in having a child by an American [though Janet did not learn this until she was 11]. She never wanted my younger, half-brother to know."

Janet thought a lot about her American father, but rather than rock this family boat, she did not try to find him until many years later. By then, she was married and had confided the secret to her daughter who became curious about the American half of her background.

A snatch of music on a radio program proved her starting point. A listener had dedicated a song to TRACE as a thank you for our help in finding their father. Janet's daughter sent for more information, which in turn brought her to us. Because Janet's father had been in the 82nd Airborne, we put her in touch with Mickey. She discovered that the G.I. had been dead for over a year.

Janet wrote to the widow in the hope that she might be willing to share some details of her father, but there was no reply. She tried again several times with no success until, once again, luck entered the equation; a letter arrived while the widow was on holiday. Her son was taking care of the mail. What Janet did not know was that he was already aware there was "someone" from his father's life living in England:

> The phone rang, "Hi, big sister! do you want me to tell you your mother's name?" I was to discover that after his father's death he had found a hidden satchel in which were photographs and letters that he had written to be forwarded to my mother via my grandparents. They returned them rather than break up what they saw as a reconciled marriage. In finding my brother and his wonderful family, I feel that I have almost got a son, he is much younger than me. He missed his father deeply and perhaps I am filling that gap. My daughter is very close to him and his wife. Our visits are wonderful.

All the fine people who offer to help are invaluable. Without them there would be many families missing out on the opportunity to enrich their lives by adding new members. I do not think that any of those mentioned above would begrudge the fact that the whole of the next chapter and parts of others are devoted to one gentleman, who thus far has dealt with more than 300 cases.

Chapter Nine

"Good Samaritan"

Philip Grinton, a retired lieutenant colonel in the U.S. Army, was on vacation in London in March 1990 when he saw an article in a British Sunday paper: "the word G.I. in the title caught my eye and the 1940s hairstyle of the girl in the photo. I have an interest in genealogy and the military." This article was headlined "British War Babes Track Their G.I. Genes." It discussed that the advances in genetic testing and counseling now meant that with the appropriate information, doctors can sometimes stop hereditary illnesses from being passed on or can at least minimize their ill effects. This can be a very important aspect of a search, especially if the searchers or their children suffer certain worrying symptoms. It is important to get across the fact that there is more than one reason why G.I. fathers need to be found.

Philip, who had been stationed in the U.K. during some of his time in service, was not a medical man but felt that he could be helpful to TRACE. He tracked me down in the local phone book, and I did the English thing and invited him to tea. This meeting was to lead to Philip becoming the "Big Daddy" of TRACE.

From the start this did not mean that all new members would be automatically passed to him. I continue to believe that with enough clues and our advice they can start on their own. It makes their eventual success all the sweeter. I constantly remind members not to use up Philip's time unnecessarily; he, like the rest of us involved with TRACE, has a life to lead. However, I am aware that whenever members of TRACE get together, his name is bandied about like a talisman, which gives him more work than is necessary. However much I insist his time should only be used as a last resort when all other possibilities are exhausted, these are grown people who do not always listen to "mother."

On one of his earliest visits to the U.K. after he became a volunteer for TRACE, I arranged for Philip to meet some members who lived close by. One of them was Anita Vellender of Middlesex who had been very upset when she discovered that the man she thought was her father was, in reality, her stepfather. She said, "I decided to go back to where my mother had lived during the war and find out as much information as I could and was told that my father's name was Randy Smith."

This, of course, is so common a name that it strikes terror into anyone beginning such a search, especially, as in Anita's case, when the G.I.'s home is unknown. Her greatest advantage was knowing the dates he was in the U.K. and the place he was based. This immediately provided a link with a successful member whose father had been on the same base. Unfortunately, and one must accept, understandably, "Smith" was not a name to lodge in anyone's mind.

Anita came to meet Philip in the hope that his access to military data unavailable to a civilian might reveal more. It did; she discovered that she was looking for the wrong man. The natural assumption that her father's name was a shortened form of Randolph was incorrect. His first name was Randley; unusual enough to narrow down the search among the Smiths.

Further investigation by Philip led to the discovery that Randley Smith had died in Opp, Alabama, in 1977. His place of death gave Anita a starting point to find her American family. She wrote to the library in Opp with a request for a copy of her father's obituary in the hope that it would provide some clues. We had learned by now that this is one of the best sources of finding surviving relatives. Anita found that she had two uncles and aunts, one of whom was called Mary, which was her middle name: "and I remembered that when I was about ten, my mother told me that during the war she had a very special friend and they called me Anita Mary after someone special."

She wrote back to the library for Aunt Mary's address. The librarian did better than that and forwarded the letter to the family. By return, Mary wrote back to ask Anita how she was connected to them. Anita said, "On my 50th birthday, I had the best present I have ever had; a letter from Mary saying that when Randley came home from overseas in 1946, he confided that he had met a lovely lady in England and they had a little girl. She signed her letter, 'your aunt Mary.'—I had found my father's family!"

In 1994, Anita went over to the States for her first visit, and while there, she phoned Philip to say that she had arrived. Without missing a beat, the family gathered around the phone to sing a chorus of thanks. While in Alabama, Anita made the emotional pilgrimage to her father's grave. This is always the most difficult part of a visit but equally the most important because when one discovers that one's father is not alive, reading the name off the stone finally brings one's search to an end, but it also makes him real.

There is a small, but important, postscript to this story. After Anita met the second branch of the Smith family, who are living in Florida, there was a discussion about Randley Smith's service medals, which he had never received. It appeared that all efforts to retrieve them had been tied up in red tape. Now, one of Anita's cousins recognized that for her they were of great importance. She took it upon herself to make a request directly to the White House. President Clinton happened to be in the press office when the call came in. Anita has now received what are her proudest possessions.

Another visitor who joined Philip and Anita that afternoon was Norma Jean Clarke from North London. Her story was in my earlier book on the subject in which she vowed that she would not give up her search for her father until the day she died. She had not been aware until she was 40 and struggling with why her father did not seem to love her that he was her mother's husband who had been away at war when she was conceived.

For a long time after the confession, her mother had professed to only remember the G.I.'s first name as "Larry." Norma appealed to the aunt who had been with her mother on that fateful date. The aunt went through her husband's wartime diary looking for names. There was only one with an initial L. The military could find no trace of him.

Norma finally persuaded her mother to remember more, and she hesitantly came up with the G.I.'s full name. This Norma brought to us; she now wanted advice from Philip on how best to pursue this. In the end, she would go through every Lawrence McCloud in the United States before finding the right one in Weaverville, California.

Philip, a native of this northern Californian area, was there to meet Norma's plane in San Francisco. He drove her up into the mountains towards her Dad's home. The first stop would be at the house of one of her brothers. From there she was on her own with her new family.

Small-town, wooden-housed, wide-open-spaced America is some-what overwhelming to someone from London. Norma did not realize that she was experiencing the same state of shock suffered by her mother's peer group when they arrived as war brides more than forty years earlier. At least she was not dumped at a deserted station; she had Philip for backup if she wanted to turn tail, but of course she did not and continued on to a rapturous reception.

On the fiftieth anniversary of the end of World War II, the book *Rich Relations* by David Reynolds was published by HarperCollins in the U.K. As one can guess, the book's title referred to the American troops who had been stationed in Britain during the war. There was brief mention of the children that the G.I.s had left behind and the fact that they were managing to find their fathers through TRACE.

This aspect of the book appeared to be what appealed most to the British press. I was bombarded with phone calls during what happened to be the busiest week of my lecture year. I was hardly available. Some of the journalists were satisfied with telephone interviews or names of a few of our successful members, but the BBC wanted me on national radio. The only time that I could spare was in Lincolnshire prior to a luncheon engagement. The BBC arranged a "down the line" interview from their local station. They, in turn, on hearing what I had to say, asked for a separate interview for local listeners. This I did after speaking at the lunch.

John Abbot who lived in nearby Mablethrope heard me in his car when he was on his way to work and wondered if he now had a chance to find his father. He had been in his late thirties when he first learned that he had a G.I. father who had no idea that he existed. He held back searching because he was concerned that other people's lives should not be disrupted, but when he heard this discussion of some of the situations on the radio, he realized for the first time that he was not unique and wrote to TRACE.

He had his father's name, but it was reasonably common as well as being beyond the alphabetical list of files saved in the St. Louis fire. We suggested a visit to the port of Southampton, which had been ringed by American troops prior to D Day. There is an enormous amount of information on those units in the reference library and that might provide some additional useful clues. Before the advent of much electronic listing, we were advising searchers to place an ad in the locator column of the appropriate service periodical. He did, but he had no response.

By now, Philip was very into computer listings, and he came up with a long list of men with John's father's name. It was up to John to deal with it. Sadly, only a few replies came back. Some returned unopened, but, before John had time to get very discouraged, the National Personnel Records Center, through alternative sources, came up with the correct service record. (No one should ever accuse them of not trying!) This did not appear to provide any new information. One has to allow for the fact that the casualty rate in the fighting meant that men moved in as replacements would not have easily been identified on paper by unit or location. More important in this case was the fact the file included a photograph of the G.I., which John sent to Philip.

Philip always examines material on fathers with a military-style fine-tooth comb and, if necessary, a magnifying glass. With that he was able to read off John's father's shoulder badge, which identified his unit as 601st Tank. This unit had a Reunion Society that confirmed Philip's find was correct.

John phoned me for advice; this close to success, panic is inevitable. As has been mentioned before, we advise writing a letter as the preferable first step. It also gives the writer an excuse to telephone later on the pretext of confirming that it has arrived. Even if it results in an immediate denial of the content, the caller has the opportunity to hear the father's voice. Pathetic as this sounds, they see it as better than nothing.

This was the route that John followed:

> I rang [him] at midnight our time. To start with, I had a guarded conversation with him, then suddenly, he said, "What is this all about?" So, I took a deep breath and told him that I thought he was my father. He then became very guarded and denied all knowledge of the things I asked him. I then rang off. I felt uncertain. When discussing this with my wife, she realised that, unlike the other Americans who had written to me, he had not wished me good luck with my search. The more we discussed the conversation, the more we were convinced he was my father.

Back he came for advice. I suggested that he write again, telling him something about himself and enclosing photographs. Almost by turnaround of mail, he had a letter back from the ex-G.I. admitting that he had known John's mother and could be his father.

Then came the following message: "11.10.95—received a telephone call from MY FATHER to say he and his wife are coming over 20 November for 11 days." The visit was a success, and John's father, a retired railroad man, came over again for his British granddaughter's wedding in 1998, and I had the opportunity to speak to him. He was a much travelled veteran, having seen action in Africa, Italy, France, and Germany, ending up in Salzburg, Austria. This indicates how difficult it would have been to find him without Philip's persistence to detail.

Another father with whom I spoke in Florida was also discovered by Philip. This G.I. had ended his war on the Italian-German border where he met and romanced a German girl. In the disruption and chaos of that time, there was no facility for marriage, but the G.I. did see his child and returned to the States where he sent long letters begging his girlfriend to join him.

The current circumstances were not conducive to transatlantic travel. Nationalities were being altered as borders were redefined. The Russians had closed off the part of Berlin where this woman had taken the child to join her parents, and she would not now desert them—but she saved the letters.

Their child, Evelyn, grew up only knowing that she had a father who lived a long way away. As she grew older, she wanted to know more about him. She took the address off the letters he had sent to her mother and wrote to him, but he was no longer in Virginia and seemed lost to her. In 1993, she saw mention of TRACE on German television. She sent us copies of those letters in the hope we could help her.

The last known area he lived in was close enough to Washington, D.C., to indicate that the G.I. might still have military or civil service connections (we always try to make a calculated guess into the unknown). So I sent the letters on to Philip. Whether this was a correct deduction is not known, but within a short time, Philip, with his more exact methods, discovered that Evelyn's father was now living in Florida.

It was now up to her to make the initial contact. The arrival of her letter was to cause a mixture of emotions. The ex-G.I. was now married and felt that after all these years, he should not disturb the status quo. His wife, who had brought a small child into the marriage and seen her husband raise her like a daughter, felt that he should respond to the letter from Germany. The American daughter's only concern was that Evelyn be kind to her "Daddy."

It was all to work out very well; Evelyn and her husband have visited Florida and been totally accepted into the family.

Not everyone is lucky enough to find their father alive. Sylvia B. of Devon was the result of a love affair between a married woman and a G.I. When her British husband returned from the war, he saw no place for this child in their home. Sylvia said, "I was initially fostered and then placed for adoption in a Church of England Home for 'Waifs and Strays.' " This name, since changed, was not seen at that time as a cruel inheritance. There was no question then of political correctness—the need was to provide a home for these unwanted children; therefore, the rules of adoption were not as stringent. Many like Sylvia suffered the consequences: "In 1946, I was placed with a couple. This turned out to be a very unhappy adoption. My adopted mother never seemed to like me. Many times she said I would be sent back where I came from because I was 'bad blood.' "

The adoptive mother had three natural children after the adoption, and her attitude deteriorated accordingly. Like many unhappy children, natural or adopted, Sylvia looked for reasons why: "one day when everyone was out, I searched for and found the tin box [where special papers were kept]. I only had a chance of a quick glance that told me that my mother's name was Dorothy and my father was an American. From that moment, my dream was to initially find 'My Mum.' "

In the next few years, Sylvia's home life became so difficult that at the age of 14, she wrote to a woman's magazine saying that she was unhappy and wanted to find her real mother. The reply (sent to a girlfriend's house) was unhelpful. Basically, it told her not to "make waves" and to forget about it. Attitudes then would have precluded giving advice on how to find a natural mother, nor were there any legal facilities available. One can assume the magazine writer thought that this was a teenage girl's fanciful dream. In any case, such publications did not expound with such forthright advice as they now do.

Sylvia ended up leaving home:

> I met my soldier husband [British] when I was 19 and married him when I was 20. Even he was warned by my adoptive mother that I was "adopted and bad blood." My husband told her it was not where I came from but where I was going. She offered me those precious papers in the tin box on my wedding day and I just couldn't take them.

Sylvia has enjoyed a very happy life, which includes her two children. Her pleasure in them may well have exacerbated the need to find her natural parents so that they could enjoy grandparent privileges. However, it was only when her adoptive mother died that she felt able to accept the paperwork, which might reveal her true identity. She hoped that finding her natural mother would in turn lead to her American father.

Unfortunately, what was handed to her contained insufficient clues. Sylvia needed to see the official copy of her adoption papers. The law by now had changed to the advantage of adopted children but required that they be counselled before any information was revealed. Throughout, she had the full support of her husband.

There was an address beside her natural mother's name, but when she called there she discovered that her mother had died. However, the homeowner had known the lady and mentioned a daughter who had visited. Sylvia found this half-sister and through her met her mother's husband—the man who had refused to keep her after his return from the war. He was now most apologetic, but meeting him triggered in her the need to find her natural father, whose name she now had from those adoption papers.

A friend who knew of the circumstances sent her a magazine cutting about TRACE. We had by this time begun to advise the use of CD-ROMs of U.S. directories, but she could find no match for her father's name. Although the G.I.'s name breached the fire-shortened list in St. Louis, we knew that by now, in some cases, they were able to find fathers through other sources, so that was the next suggested step.

Since it was a proven fact that it was good therapy to link up members who either were searching in a similar area or lived near each other, we put Sylvia on to someone with whom she could pool notes. This TRACE member went further and suggested a direct approach to Philip (something we were still holding in reserve): "I couldn't believe it when, in Philip's reply, he had found three men with my father's name and their Social Security numbers. He advised me to write again to the National Personnel Records Office in St. Louis quoting the Freedom of Information Act."

Philip's magic wand is a combination of computer information, a splash of military knowledge, and the authority of his position in the U.S. Army that enables him to use the correct buzzwords. For this, we are all truly grateful.

This time, Sylvia was informed by the NPRC that her father had died twelve years earlier: "the loss of my Mum had somehow prepared me for the fact that my Dad could have died too, but that fact that I will never be able to see or touch either, I think will always hurt a little."

The search was not over because Philip found someone he was sure was the G.I.'s widow. Sylvia was concerned not to hurt a family who might know nothing of this episode in her father's life. She phoned me and we talked it through. I suggested that we had found that with time people mellow and she should try a carefully worded letter. She said, "I was certainly not prepared for what happened next. I received this wonderful letter from Dallas. A gentleman called Wren Worley who told me that he was my father's dearest friend and that he was sure that I was his daughter."

This was the start of a series of letters in which Sylvia learned that her father's widow had died. His eldest daughter had received the letter and sent it to her "Uncle Wren," who had always been close to the family. He now became Sylvia's link with her father. With the first photograph of him that she received, she saw the strong resemblance between him and her son.

To date, only one of her father's American children has fully accepted her; this is not unusual. They cannot always be expected immediately to adjust to this hidden side of their father's life. Sylvia continues to be hopeful that they will eventually see that all she wants from them is love, recognition, and a share of their memories.

Fortunately, her father's best friend has not only filled in some of the gaps but invited her over to visit him and his wife:

Monday, 23rd March [1998] I stepped from the plane into the warmest welcome anyone could have. Wren, his wife and their daughter were waiting all smiles with my name on a placard! From then on it was non-stop love and affection. I learned so much about my wonderful Dad. Everyone seemed to have loved him. I was told by a close friend, "your father lived the American dream of hard work and success." More important to me though was that I now know I look out from his eyes, have his hands and feet—even walk like him. I felt very much at home and in some ways, it seemed I had known them all my life. I will never be able to thank these wonderful people enough for making my Dad come to life. Now he is real to me, my "jigsaw" is complete. I feel that I have been adopted again but for all the right reasons.

Wren has since sent Sylvia the history of his friendship with her father, starting with when they met at college and their later good fortune in making contact with each other while in Germany in World War II.

One of Philip's detailed, ongoing situations is in conjunction with a very determined woman searching on behalf of herself and her twin brother. While we are aware that some people fade away when the going gets tough, I doubt that Angela W. of Monmouth, Wales, will ever give up. With Philip's help, she has learned her father's

Army unit. The next step was to visit the archives in Haverfordwest where he had met her mother who was also in uniform (British) to see what records they might have on his unit.

Angela's late start in this search had been caused by the fact that up to the last few years, her adoptive mother had been against it. This delay means that people she is approaching for clues are very old and have unreliable memories. Another obstacle has been the fact that the office holding her adoptive papers has been reluctant to let her see them. This must indicate that each district holds to its own rules and regulations.

Undeterred, Angela by now has enough information from those archives to build up a picture of the period when her parents met. The local paper had reported on a Thanksgiving party the American troops had given for schoolchildren in the area. She took the names of the G.I.s mentioned and sent them to Philip. From this he was able to establish that the only troops in Haverfordwest in December 1944 were the 291st Infantry, en route to Europe: "my mother told me she only knew him for about six weeks. The time factor fits. She also told me that he was a low-ranking officer. Philip said, in that case he would be listed in the Official Army Register."

She was given a contact name of someone at the British Library in London who had done searches for Philip in the past (his genealogical interest goes beyond G.I. fathers). This person has agreed to undertake the task. It has yet to be completed. There is one provocative clue; Angela's father was nicknamed "Red." While there were a large number of "Reds" in the U.S. forces (I married one), this particular one might like to know that he has a red-headed granddaughter in Wales.

Another adopted G.I. child assisted by Philip is John Santy from Birmingham, in the British Midlands. His adoptive parents were very strict and did not tell him that he was the child of a G.I. One should point out that at this period G.I.s' children were suspect because one did not know enough of their background. In spite of his adoptive parents' precautions, John learned about himself on the school playground at age 9. At that young age, such news may not have much importance. No further mention was made until the year before he was to be married, when an aunt took it upon herself to fill him in on his mother's maiden name and his father's name and rank. As his adoptive parents had still not revealed to him the fact that he was adopted, John decided not to pursue the situation.

It would not be until 1986 that he felt a need to find his roots and sent for his original birth certificate. This showed his natural mother's name, but there was no mention of his father. He managed to track his mother down and learned that she had consistently refused to reveal the father's full name. She only admitted that he had had the rank of colonel (she herself had been an officer in the British Women's Army). She did, however, give John a photograph of his father.

For nine years, he wrote to U.S. organizations and government departments for any clues as to the identity of his father. With no surname to offer, it was an impossible task even though a couple of military magazines printed his picture with a request for information. In 1995, he heard about TRACE.

As has been mentioned before, many people approach us with flimsy, not to say sparse, evidence that can consist of just a nickname. This is even more frustrating for them if it is accompanied by a photograph, though, as has been demonstrated, Philip can sometimes pinpoint a clue from the uniform. Much to his frustration, in this case, the photograph yielded nothing. John was advised to return to his natural mother:

> In May of 1996, I decided to have one last try writing to my mother. (She had previously said she wanted nothing to do with me.) A few days later, I was astonished to receive the information from her with the proviso that I did not contact her again. The most fortunate part was that it turned out to be a most unusual surname. I came up with only 10 listings in the whole of U.S.A.

These were sent to Philip, but none of these people had details that matched John's father. As a last resort, Philip sent a copy of the photograph to the ten addresses with a letter asking if the man was known to them. After the usual agonizing delay, Philip received a phone call from a person who turned out to be John's half-brother. The sad news was that the colonel was dead; the good news was that this half-brother often had business reasons to visit the U.K. and would like to meet John: "Philip suggested that I ring him right away which I did although I had to sit down, I felt physically unwell, overwhelmed to have it come together after 11 years."

Subsequently, John met his half-brother and wife who came for a short visit. His half-sister and her husband came over, too, for what proved to be a very emotional reunion. A dinner was arranged in a private room of their hotel:

> We had a wonderful evening. My brother brought me my father's insignia and my sister had prepared a folder with the family tree, photographs and newspaper cuttings. My sister

who is now retired would like us to visit them for a holiday. They have all accepted me totally and they are such nice people, so easy to get along with. It has taken a very long time for me to reach this happy ending and unfortunately I shall never meet my father but I now know what an outstanding soldier he was and very respected. My brother has since given me more of his insignia and one of his medals which I shall treasure. One of my first visits when I go to U.S.A. is to see my father's grave at Arlington Cemetery.

I am sure that when Philip read about TRACE in the British newspaper he did not anticipate that one phone call to me in March 1990 would expand in quite this way. However, I know how much he enjoys the challenge and the satisfaction he shares at our successes, so I have recently sent him a new conundrum to solve.

Hilary W., from Stoke-on-Trent, has done extensive searches, but with the minute information of where her father was stationed, a photograph but no name, and that he came from Buffalo, New York, she still has a problem. She refuses to give up, so with Philip's help she may yet be met again before this book ends.

Chapter Ten

"Welcome Home"

To become an American citizen is not necessarily on the agenda when people embark on the search for their G.I. fathers or families. Some, once it is all over, are totally satisfied to have fit in that last piece of their personal jigsaw, happy that their "half-American" claim is justified. They can now go on with their lives. Not all of them can afford the fare to the States, though we do urge them to borrow if necessary to get there rather than suffer the inevitable regrets. One early member serves as an example of the danger of delay. She was saving up so that all her family could go together. Her father died before this could be accomplished.

Some, in finding their father, fulfill either a lifetime need of knowing that they really belong in the States or see citizenship as their right. Newly found fathers are quick to urge their child to become a "Yank." Invariably, our newly made American members of TRACE proudly send us a copy of their new passport.

Michael James Lee may be Jimmy Ward, Jr., to his Dad in the U.S., but he has to use his birth name on his American passport. Between frequent business trips, he spends as much time as he can with his father and family. They would all be happy if he stayed forever, but like many of those G.I. children, there is a strong loyalty to the country where he has spent most of his life. This does not preclude these G.I. children from wishing to confirm their American identity.

Michael's citizenship was a simple matter of his very happy father signing the necessary papers. Not all have come to their citizenship that easily and, in several cases, it has had to be fought for.

Norma Jean Clarke of London, who has been previously mentioned in this book as counselor to the less positive or distressed newly enrolled members, is one of them. In celebration of her citizenship, she has hyphenated her father's name to hers and is now Norma Jean Clarke-McCloud: "Back in 1989 and still incessantly searching for my father, we flew to America for the first time. I felt annoyed that as I was part American, I should have the long wait at Immigration."

Once Norma found her father, with his encouragement, she began to investigate how she could become an American citizen. The complication lay in the fact that her mother had been married at the time of her conception. This may have provided her with cover when she had the G.I.'s child but left Norma with complications. Her stepfather, who she thought was her father until she turned 40, was named on her birth certificate.

In spite of the fact that she had affidavits from her natural father, his sons and daughter, all ready to claim her, this proved an immovable obstacle. Since by then, her mother had died and could not be a witness, the final proof rested on when Norma's stepfather had served overseas. Norma could only get a copy of the appropriate military records to back up her claim with his permission. He refused. One must note here that this was motivated by stubbornness, not a refusal to lose his claim on a daughter. He had always been a reluctant father; now that Norma's mother was dead, there was no need to keep up the pretense. But, one has also to accept that having agreed to keep this G.I. "cuckoo" in his nest, he may now have seen no reason why he should supply proof that she was not his daughter.

The relationship deteriorated even further as he demanded she return his wartime medals:

I had them from before when I believed that he was my father. Now he wrote and said, "if you want war medals, ask your father in America for his!" He signed his full signature. I took this letter to the Embassy with all the other papers. The Embassy sent them to Washington. Two weeks later, they called; "you have your citizenship, it only took two weeks. The quickest one we have ever known."

Norma-Jean first used that precious passport in 1997 when visiting her aunt who had been a war bride (the one whose G.I. husband had introduced Norma's mother to her father):

> As we arrived at New York Airport [JFK], I saw the long queues waiting to go through Immigration. I told an official that I was an American citizen but my children were British. She signalled me to go straight to the U.S. side with them. The official took my U.S. passport (my stomach was going over and over). He looked at it and said, "Welcome Home." I had tears in my eyes as I floated out of the airport.

Patricia Plant was 16 when she discovered that her father was a G.I. It happened as she overheard an argument between her stepfather and pregnant mother regarding the fact that their coming baby would at least not be a "Yank." Since this man had been unkind to her, Patricia was glad to know that they were not really related.

She was, at that age, too young to embark on any search, nor did there seem any point when her grandparents suggested that her father had possibly been killed in the war. Eventually, Patricia's mother filled her in on the circumstances of her birth and produced photographs of the G.I. Like many of her contemporaries in this kind of situation, rather than "make waves" between her mother and stepfather, she waited until her mother's death.

Her application for help to the U.S. Embassy in 1992 was responded to with a list of people and organizations who might help. This included the address of TRACE. We did not question Patricia's information, which listed her father as coming from Chicago until international directory inquiries did not have him listed there. Since Harold Ludwig, one of our earliest helpers, had been stationed in the same area as her father, we suggested that she contact him. For once, he could not help since her father was not in his unit and that particular county had been overcrowded with G.I.'s prior to the invasion of France.

The next step was the National Personnel Records Center in St. Louis. When they sent her her father's last know state, it turned out to be Iowa, not Illinois; both would have sounded similar to British ears at that time. More encouraging was the fact that as she was only sent the State, not her father's full address, it meant that he was still alive. In a search that lasted a year and for a while went out of state to Yorktown, South Dakota, Patricia finally found her father in Sioux City, Iowa. He was delighted to welcome her into the family: "In 1994, Dad had his name put on my birth certificate. I became a U.S. Citizen at the American Embassy in London where my search had begun."

Since then, Patricia has visited her father eleven times, and he has been to England to meet her family as have her American siblings.

Donald Wilson of Ipswich has finally learned what his life would have been like if his mother had followed his father to the States. Don is a 1950s baby, proving that the conclusion of World War II did not bring a halt to G.I.s romancing European girls nor marrying them. Don grew up knowing that he had an American father who was supposed to be living in Washington state. The more important details that would enable him to be located were not revealed until his mother died.

The distance between father and son seemed prohibitive; Don employed a private investigator. TRACE has always tried to discourage members from following such a path. It is not that we disapprove of their methods, but we feel that such people operate better on a more personal basis. All Don received was a printout of people named D. B. Wilson in the United States, something he could have obtained himself from a CD-ROM of U.S. directories.

Patience is never a virtue once people decide to look for their fathers. While waiting to hear back from the NPRC in St. Louis, Don accessed the Internet for family history searching. A. D. Wilson was found in California, but he had died in 1985. When Don received the death certificate, to his relief, the middle initial was incorrect; the search was still ongoing.

The response from St. Louis finally came but was confusing. They gave Nevada as the last known state of residence for Don's father. To try to clarify the situation, he contacted the wife of his parents' best man and, doing the inevitable "off in all directions" action which is representative of new members of TRACE, also sought help from a Mormon couple he had befriended who were now returning to the west coast: "they telephoned on my behalf and talked to my father. He was overjoyed at the news and so was his wife. I called later and spoke to both of them. He was thrilled that he was a grandfather. He has no other children." Don was to discover that his father had retired from his work in Nevada, which explained the confusion over the last known address. Like many of his contemporaries he had "gone home" and was now living in a small town back in Washington State. Don immediately organized a visit:

We covered 3,700 miles in 9 days. Visited the bar, restaurant that my father ran in Nevada; all the way up to Colfax where, if Mum had followed to the States, I would have lived. We visited my grandparents' grave, the house where my father lived, his school. We were in Oregon along the Columbia river, and as they loved shooting they took me out to have a go in the gravel pits and were surprised that I was a good shot (or lucky). It was a great time had by all. His wife Ruth is a lovely lady, doing a great job looking after my father. Ruth said, out of earshot that this meeting had made my father's life complete. It's great to have a father. I've had two stepfathers in my time but I could never, even at an early age, call them other than their first name. So, it's great to at last call somebody, "Dad."

From early on in this visit, the G.I. ventured tentative questions to Don as to whether he would consider permanently residing in the States. While he is immensely proud of his American birthright, Don is now too tied to the U.K. by family and business to consider more than frequent trips to the United States.

Don met his father in the early summer of 1998, and before fall had arrived, his father had signed the papers that confirmed that his newly found son was an American. Don used his new passport for the first time when he took his son over to meet his American grandpa.

Vance Pennington of Surrey overheard that his father was an American at an early age: "What really registered was the word, 'real'; that the bullying, cruel man who forced me to call him, 'Dad' was not who he pretended to be." He learned more during another parental quarrel that involved the fact that financial assistance for him from the States had ceased. This included a threat to contact the authorities in Indiana, and this was how Vance learned the name of his father's home state.

From an early age, he determined to escape his unhappy environment. The decision was made for him when he was removed from school at 16 and sent out to support himself. He lived in a small bed-sit, enhanced by a large map of the United States on one wall. Just before his seventeenth birthday, Vance decided to approach the American Embassy for help: "I am not really sure what I expected to gain from this but the result was extremely disappointing; I didn't get past the doorman, let alone the opportunity to discuss this with someone of authority."

He began to grasp at flimsy clues, such as the same name as his father coming up on a TV credit. He would write for help but rarely received a reply. He said, "friends and work colleagues began to learn of my plight and often a visitor to U.S.A. would bring me back a page from a telephone directory. My father was out there and I was going to find him."

Many years and thousands of letters passed, and by February 1982, Vance realized that he was getting nowhere. Friends suggested the obvious answer was to persuade his mother to accompany him to the American Embassy. She might not be willing to confide in him, but it was possible she would respond to someone in an official capacity. While she refused the request, it made her recognize the importance her son attached to his background. She surprised him by producing the divorce papers from her first marriage, which cited the G.I. as co-respondent.

Vance thought he now had all the paperwork needed to further his claim for citizenship, but it did not prove that simple. He received a lengthy reply from the Embassy, part of which indicated, "it has been determined that children born of American servicemen and Alien mothers out of wedlock, do not have and never have the right to American citizenship. Should you ever wish to visit the United States, you will have to apply for a visa."

Vance was devastated; this he was sure was another attempt to put him off. He did not realize yet that this situation could be overturned if he found his father or family who would be willing to sign the necessary papers.

For twelve more years, he continued to write to anyone he found in the United States who had the name Pennington. Aware of this, his mother recognized how determined her son was and began to fill him in on her romance with the G.I. She provided his service number and the base where he had served. One has to accept that her earlier reticence probably related to the fact that she was of a generation for whom divorce was socially unacceptable. Worse yet was the fact that one of the few grounds was adultery, not then exactly what one would expect of a lady!

Up till now, Vance was only in possession of a shortened form of his birth certificate, which did not need to show the father's name. In his case, it was an obvious avoidance of the truth because when he applied for the original, his father's name was on it. He was now confident that with this and his mother's divorce papers, the American Embassy would be satisfied. This determination to become an American stems from a need to restore his self-esteem. He had grown up feeling downgraded by his illegitimacy, which was exacerbated by a disparaging step-father. Back came the reply that he had been praying for: "it appears from the documents that you have supplied that you may have the right to American citizenship."

The operative word in the letter was "may." Vance returned to the American Embassy to find out how this could be finalized; it rested on him finding his father. They furnished him with a list of options on how this might be accomplished. The most logical appeared to be the National Personnel Records Center. They notified him that his father's files had perished in the fire. He then approached TRACE.

Our advice was to start with the Veterans Administration in the state of Indiana since he knew there was some connection there. While waiting, he followed up on another list of people with his father's last name. One responded with the suggestion that he try the Pennington Research Association. Before he could pursue this, a reply came from the special affairs officer of the VA in Indiana:

> They had found various documents bearing my father's name which indicated that he had returned to Southern Indiana in 1946 promising to send for my mother. More documentation arrived from the late 40s between the American Embassy and a solicitor [lawyer] acting for my mother which showed that maintenance payments were forthcoming and therefore proved his recognition of me. A further letter arrived with two U.S. birth certificates; I had a brother and sister across the Pond.

Eager to share part of his father's life when he was in the U.K., Vance made a visit to his base at Great Ashfield in Suffolk. A friendly villager filled him in on his father's unit and its location. Vance said, "I set off for the farmhouse and the owner of the land which had been the home of the 385th Heavy Bombardment Group. From him I learned that there was a London based man who had an interest in WW II aircraft nose art and a vast database of the crews." This gentleman put Vance in touch with Joan Peterson, our helper in Ohio. He had already been given Bud Shapard as a contact, but he now felt that Ohio was the closest to Indiana and it was not fair to take up two people's time. He would pin his hopes on Joan. This has led to a lasting friendship, and Vance has visited her a couple of times. As all TRACE helpers are in touch with each other, exchanging useful data, Joan also suggested that Philip Grinton be sent the military details, and this became a team play. Within a week, Philip passed on the news that the G.I. was dead; he had actually taken his own life in 1972: "Devastation is an inadequate word. Despair doesn't even come near. I have still to recover from the realisation that I will never get to know my Dad. Never would I have a chance to hear his voice or feel his embrace."

Philip was able to send Vance a copy of his father's death certificate. He learned that he had been buried in Superior, Wisconsin, with full military honors. Vance clung to the strangely comforting thought that this suicide may have been activated by guilt about those he had left in England. This feeling would be justified when he later learned of the unsettled life his father had led on his return to the States.

Now Vance determined to find his siblings. A copy of the obituary sent by the chief librarian in Superior listed three. He wrote back and asked if there were Penningtons in that area: "within a short space of time, I received his reply; 'rather than send you the list, I took it upon myself to make a few phone calls on your behalf. I have found your brother, Rob.' "

I must put in a personal word of thanks here for the many librarians all over the United States who have responded so positively and directed searchers on to their surviving families.

His brother made Vance welcome. He now visits him and his family every year. From that first discovery, everything began to come together, including meetings with his other siblings, cousins, and "stepmother." Added to that, when finally Vance contacted the Pennington Research Association, they sent him his family history which dates back to early settlers in Virginia in the seventeenth century.

Now it was even more important for him to persist with his dream of becoming an American: "My application was long and complicated. I had to explain my reasons for wanting citizenship. They wanted all the details of my life and my search. . . . my application with evidence of maintenance payments was unique. On April 27 1995, I was awarded citizenship of the United States of America as a right of birth. It was the proudest day of my life."

Sandy Peacham of Camberley, Surrey, started life with complications. She was adopted by someone within the family and grew up knowing her real mother as an aunt. She was, however, told the truth about being adopted and the fact that her father had been in the U.S. Navy stationed at Dartmouth, Devon, during World War II. Her search became so detailed that it could fill a book; what follows will only be the highlights.

Sandy started looking for her father in 1960, but, in spite of her paying private detectives, made no progress. As the years passed and laws changed towards investigating the background of an adoption, she was advised to seek help first from an official counselor. She preferred to stay independent. She felt with knowing her father's name it was just a question of finding him. She should have recognized that problems might occur because the family reported that once her father discovered her mother was pregnant, he backed away: "his friends and Commanding Officer were disgusted with him after all the hospitality that had been given to him and his comrades. Even one of his friends offered to marry Edna [her natural mother]." There is, however, some evidence that contradicts this and indicates that Sandy's father did want to marry her mother. She was the one who did not wish to be tied down and chose to have the baby in a home for unmarried mothers in Exeter, Devon.

By the time Sandy joined TRACE in 1989, she had written to hundreds of departments trying to define what branch of the U.S. Navy her father was in. Meanwhile an aunt told her that he came from Alabama, so she had an alternative starting point. Sandy found two phone numbers there that matched her father's name and came to us for advice on how to use them.

It has been noted before that we discourage people from making phone calls. Emotion gets in the way of keeping to a straight script. It may be longer but is a less stressful start on both sides if one sends a letter of inquiry. Neither person Sandy contacted was the one she was looking for.

She decided to take a different direction and investigated the wartime history of the Port of Dartmouth in an effort to discover which units of the U.S. Navy were there at that time. She "eventually found out that he was probably, but only maybe, with the Naval advanced Amphibious Base and part of the Naval Construction Batallion there (SeaBees). Over all these years of writing and phoning people with his name—and there are hundreds all over America—and 3 Presidents, Chat Show hosts including Oprah Winfrey and Rikki Laine [*sic*], all to no avail."

At this stage, Sandy had no service number, let alone a last known address. This was what thwarted her attempts to get further official details and proved most exasperating:

> All through the years of writing to the U.S. Naval departments and Government offices it was always the same procedure. You write and ask if they have any information on this particular person, giving name, Service and state. They reply by sending you a form to fill out. This asks for his service number, date of birth etc. Surely common sense should tell them that if you had all or even some of it you would not be contacting them in the first place, so really, the U.S. side of things put you up against a brick wall.

In 1996, Sandy accepted the sense of talking to an adoption counselor. This long overdue act opened what had been a closed door. She was presented with papers that showed her father's signature on his agreement relating to her adoption and his 1944 address.

She was back searching in Alabama and wrote to the Birmingham library for some assistance. Their research produced information that not only included who had lived at that address (her grandfather) but the details of his obituary, which revealed that Sandy had two uncles and an aunt and gave the aunt's address and telephone number.

Things began to look promising, especially since Charles Pellegrini at the NPRC, who had been sent a copy of those adoption papers, now came back with her father's service number, record, and last known address. She was informed that they would forward a letter to her father on her behalf, if she wished.

A letter coming from an official source has a better chance of being accepted and possibly will pass by a curious wife without being opened and causing a domestic crisis. This letter was accepted and signed for but not in the name of Sandy's father. She tried again, this time with two letters, one addressed to her father and one to the person named on the receipt. Both came back "undeliverable."

Sandy thought perhaps this aunt for whom she had an address might prove more amenable. Without completely revealing her identity she managed to persuade the aunt to forward a letter to her nephew. Sandy then did the usual follow-up routine of a phone call to ensure it had arrived: "My aunt said that she had received my letter and burned it. The next day, I received one from her daughter pointing out that the lady was 90 years old and found the phone calls upsetting and that legal action would be taken if I did not desist."

Sandy wrote and apologized, admitted who she was, and enclosed copies of her paperwork to prove it. She heard no more, but stored in her mind were the details of that first conversation with the aunt, which included the fact her father had gone to the coast to visit a brother who was ill. Examining a map convinced her that "the coast" was Florida. Her hunch was confirmed when she found someone with her father's last name living there.

Her uncle was more responsive to her letter and promised to contact his brother about her. When he phoned back he was most apologetic and said that his brother denied all knowledge of Sandy; he said it was a long time ago and he could not remember. In spite of that, the uncle said he would not let the matter rest there and if Sandy would send him copies of those adoption papers, he would present them to his brother. She decided to include a photograph of herself and her daughters in the envelope to confirm a likeness in the hope that, as has happened in the past, the sight of grandchildren would prove the greatest temptation. There was an agonizing wait of three weeks, and the reply that came back contained a complete change of attitude: "Please be advised that under no cir-cumstances would we like to be contacted about the enclosed mat-ter."

Sandy visited her natural mother to talk through this rejection and discovered fuller details of the relationship that had led to her conception. The couple had gone together for eighteen months, her father had become a friend of the family, and in spite of his refusal to marry the mother (or possibly the reverse) he had visited Sandy as a baby.

This made her father's present refusal to accept her even more frustrating. To satisfy herself that she definitely had the right man, Sandy wrote to Charles Pellegrini in St. Louis to see if she could have a copy of his signature to compare with the one on her adoption papers. They matched. Angry at this continued denial, she wrote to Jefferson County, Alabama, to see if her father could be forced to take a paternity test. The answer was negative.

She saw only one last resort—a letter to her father. These excerpts from that letter actually encompass the feelings of all the people who embark on this kind of search:

> I realize that from the reply I received last month from your brother that you do not want anything to do with me, but I feel that after trying for almost 36 years to make some form of con-tact, I just cannot sit back and give up now.
>
> You and your brother knew your parents. I never had that privilege. I was rejected as a child over 50 years ago, and it would appear that I am again being rejected. What have I done wrong? I never asked to be born in that awful time of World War II. I have never held anything against you about the situ-ation or the circumstances of that time. . . . If something very hurtful happened between you and my mother, I would like to know and understand. If this is the case, am I still being blamed and penalized for events that I really had nothing to do with?
>
> There are many questions both personal and medical I need to know. I have never asked for much out of life but I do have some sort of rights to know about my roots and background. . . . Whatever anyone says, I am half-American.

There is a fascinating twist to this tale. Sandy Peacham is now fully American. The paperwork she had collected to prove her case to her father was accepted by the American Embassy as her right to become an American citizen. Her father's country has accepted her, but to date he has not. With the fact that father and daughter seem to match in genetic tenacity, one can assume that she will not give up until he does!

A different example of tenacity comes from Linda of Liverpool. Early in her search she discovered that her father was dead; she was five months too late. This made it all the more important to find out something about him, but the two half sisters she located would not respond. Unwilling to accept this rejection as a complete cut off of the American half of her family, Linda determined to continue her search.

After several years, she located a cousin in Boston. The bonus was the fact that he had been close to her father, and he became a prime source of information. A family gathering was arranged at which time Linda was presented with some precious mementos, which included her father's hunting gun: "I just stood there, sliding my hands over it and got a feeling of comfort."

In celebration, Linda has adopted her father's last name. She brought back to England his watch and cigarette lighter. "It was very poignant to think that my Dad had actually worn the watch and used the lighter for many years. In that moment of deep thought, I held them and felt very close to him. It was almost as though he was standing by my side watching over me."

As touching were the letters from her father to the family, which her aunt gave her to keep. In them, he had written about her mother. Linda said:

> Since I have been aware that my Dad was an American, I had very much wanted to adopt dual nationality and hold not only my British passport but also an American one. The red tape involved in the process has been never ending, but now, thanks to my cousin who has supplied me with legal documentation as to my being a legitimate member of the family, and confirming that my Dad was indeed Mid-Russo, this should hopefully speed up my application.

From this, one could safely assume that Linda would be the next in line for official approval of her claim to an American heritage. It came through; as of October 1999 she is now an American citizen.

Chapter Eleven

꒰ ꒷꒦ ꒷ ꒰

"Letters from America"

Besides the "thank you" notes that we receive from fathers, there are other fathers or their families in the States who write in the hope that we can help them make contact with a child that was left behind. These usually arrive after any mention of our work has been in the U.S. press (and now on the Internet).

Some requests go beyond our capability, like one that came in from a woman in Ohio. She wrote to complain that the children of her marriage had turned out "rotten" and since her husband thought that he had left one behind during his wartime duty in the U.K., could we possibly find him or her? Always willing to help, I asked for further details—something basic like where the G.I. met this British woman. The reply was, "in a Pub in London." We do have lots of members whose mothers met their G.I. fathers in a pub, not always in London; they usually have the name and the location. Since there are thousands of pubs in London, we could not take this inquiry any further.

Nor could we be of much help to a man in Michigan who sent a desperate, six-line letter wanting to know if he had any children in England. I can only assume that he enjoyed several romances and was now hopeful that the result of at least one of them might have applied to TRACE. One also suspects that he was at the stage of his life where he was lonely as much as repentant. He may end up being lucky; Sophie Byrne, our membership secretary, has a phenomenal memory and will either recall the connection or save the name in case it appears on a new member's application form.

In general, we have found that matching fathers to children is not as easy as the reverse procedure. We run a very unsophisticated operation. We have neither the time nor the funds to get involved in an electronic filing system that would allow for cross-indexing, but our basic methods do not appear to inhibit the success rate.

When it comes to the reverse method of identification, children are not as easy to find because so many people were displaced by the war. As noted from the case histories previously mentioned, mothers in uniform could have been transferred or left the services to have the child in obscurity or had the child adopted. If the mother of the child was a civilian, she could have been bombed out of her home or, in some cases, become a fatal casualty.

To this must be added the fact that in the immediate postwar years, a large number of people emigrated to places like Australia and New Zealand; it was a perfect way for an unmarried mother to start a new life. This explains why we have a thriving group of European-born members in that part of the globe.

In spite of such difficulties, when letters come from America with details of where the couple met or the sweetheart lived, this does provide a starting point. If they are not at the address, someone may provide the new location. We also try to persuade the local press to participate but have found that they do not always relate to the emotion attached to the request, so it becomes a matter of luck as to whether the story appeals.

We are also approached to track down offspring of broken marriages, where the war bride returned to the U.K. with the child and then cut off all connection. Even if the details are out of date, we have learned by now that there is always a chance, especially if the story gets some publicity. In one such case, when the Manchester Lancashire newspaper ran the story, it was seen by an old friend of the mother. She reported back that the daughter was now living in the States. She was, after all an American by right of her parents' marriage. She and her father have been reunited.

Sadly, another gentleman in Pennsylvania has not been as fortunate so far, despite a postwar marriage which should be advantageous. The paperwork and records would not have been in danger of destruction by bombing. In this case, the G.I. serving in the U.K. took his British wife back to the States. The reasons why she returned to Ipswich, Suffolk, are not clear. She has since remarried. He wants to make contact with their daughter, who he last saw when she was fifteen months old.

A letter that came from Missouri surprised me by being written in

German. The writer was seeking a child born in Germany in April 1946. This is an impossibly wide canvass to cross without details, but when Inge Gurr wrote for them, there was no reply. One can only suspect that, once again, the acronym TRACE led them to think we are an agency in business to find people. Once such applicants discover that it is only useful advice and encouragement that we offer, they tend to bow out. This is their loss; being part of this group can provide unexpected benefits. These kind of requests go into our newsletter. From it can come success, such as the aunt in Florida who found her British niece, who had given up her search after she found that her father was dead. Now she has a family who want to claim her, and she is being filled in on her Dad. Since it is also becoming clear that some children of the unfound G.I.s have emigrated to the States, one hopes that they might respond to this book.

Some of the letters that we receive from American children are from before or after their fathers' wartime service. They have either confided about their European child or as has been mentioned before, when some veterans die, hidden photographs and letters relating to their wartime romances are discovered.

One woman in Pennsylvania knows that her father joined the Merchant Marines to return to the U.K. to find his girlfriend and their daughter but was unsuccessful. This American daughter would now like to make up for lost time on his behalf. He was in the 29th Bomber Division, 8th Air Force, stationed in the Northampton area. So far, a feature in the local paper has had no response.

Someone in Utah may have a better chance, as the circumstances are fifteen years more recent. The G.I. fell in love with a girl who worked in a Munich bakery; he signed responsibility for their child, Sylvia, and put in a request to marry the mother. In 1960, before this could take place, he was posted back to the United States. His youngest American daughter wants to make him happy by finding this eldest child. The only suggestion that I could offer was to try to interest a newspaper in Munich, but I have heard nothing more.

One has to accept that there are many occasions where the old European flame burned out waiting and has gone on with her life, possibly covering up all evidence of the earlier romance. The American man may no longer be seen as the desired one who got away or may be expected to stay a fond memory. I had a letter from an ex-G.I. who hoped to find a family that he had befriended and one sister in particular. Sensing a potential for romance, the local paper ran the story. This was followed by a frantic phone call from another sister. None of them welcomed this intrusion, and the G.I.'s old girlfriend did not want her marriage disrupted.

A more promising letter came from Sue H. in Virginia who, after the death of her father, received confidences from her mother about his "indiscretions" while in England in World War II:

> Mom said she had a picture of a little girl with her mother [but now she had conveniently misplaced it]. The more I thought about having a sister, the more curious I became about her. I want to know if she knew about Dad, did he send presents over the years, did she have contact with him like I suspect she did? I have a feeling that there were letters between Dad and Denise's mother. The biggest motivation was that I loved and missed my father so very much that I wanted to find some other part of him. I remembered my parents having some "discussions" about someone named Denise. I remembered Dad asking me, when I was about 6 or 7, if I would like to have a sister, that he knew how we could get one but we had to talk Mom into this idea.

One can empathize with "Mom's" quandary. While we have had occasions when the American wife has welcomed this extra child into the family, it is more likely to be after considerably more time than this has elapsed.

Sue came to TRACE via a circuitous route, which included a television program that referred her to Transatlantic Brides and Parents Association, a group formed by the parents of the original British brides at a time when the cost of transatlantic travel was still prohibitive. There were enough war brides in the States by then to organize the more affordable block bookings in either direction. Membership now is a more social affair, with a mix of the original war brides and other European ex-pats.

Sue had already made contact with the British Embassy and Social Security U.K. in the hope of finding a child registered in her father's name during the first half of 1945. We managed to get her story in a paper local to the area where her father was stationed, but there was no response.

Sue is in possession of her father's military records obtained from St. Louis, which include hospital admission cards. Through these she learned that he had been wounded during the invasion of France and brought back to England to the 316th Station Hospital, one of the several military hospitals that had been set up in the U.K. to receive casualties. This one was in Teingrace, Devon.

She is assuming this is where, once recovered, he romanced one of the nurses. However, the location does not necessarily provide a clue to where that nurse actually lived or had the baby. Women called into any kind of uniformed service during the war were rarely stationed close to home. Therefore, Sue cannot assume that her half-sister was born nearby. If the mother had had understanding parents, she might have been able to return to them with her "problem." Given the social disapproval of unmarried motherhood, if she did so, some sort of story might have been concocted, which might not now be easy to unravel. Other choices were adoption or a change of identity, all of which make the ultimate discovery of such a child more difficult. This Sue is finding out because she has now searched through microfiches of births in the area of the hospital and has yet to find a newborn named Denise. Since this would not have been a common first name of that period, this should be of some help, but should the child have subsequently been given up for adoption, there may have been a later name change to something less "foreign." However, if any reader recognizes this story about a 1st sergeant, Company B, 359, 90th Infantry Division, Sue would be delighted to make contact.

Lynn C. in Alabama has not had such a cooperative mother when it comes to details about her father's off-duty history while serving overseas. Her father was actually British born and became a legal U.S. citizen by virtue of his wartime duty in the U.S. Army. He was an early arrival in the U.K. and would have stood out even more than the others because he was a G.I. with a British accent:

> Some time after my father's death in 1970, my mother found letters in our house from a woman in England my father had had an affair with during WW II. My mother was quite upset, the letters came over the years to where he worked. I think there must have been a child, otherwise, why write to a man with a family half a world away? If there is a child for a Dad with light red hair and blue eyes, he or she has two brothers and two sisters here in the States.

Since we are often offered such flimsy evidence without a name by people who approach TRACE, this letter is worth including. The details it contains may help identify this particular father.

Another Lynne who lives in Pennsylvania is trying to find a British cousin: "we recently discovered that my uncle, Gilbert Duran fathered a child while stationed in Great Britain in WW II. We think it was a son. Unfortunately, uncle died young. His mother, my grandmother made mention of this child only shortly before she died last year. This person would be my uncle's only child. We think this woman kept in contact for a while."

Lynne read about TRACE in an article in the *Philadelphia Inquirer*. She was moved to make contact with us because she felt badly that her uncle would have left his only child behind. We have seen evidence of situations like this, leaving such a residue of guilt that the G.I. has either never married or, in extreme cases, committed suicide. This family is trying to make up for their uncle's lost time: "Gilbert is survived by three half-sisters and several nieces and nephews. We have pictures and memories to share along with some medical history." The latter could be the most important reason why this child of the war should be found. Lack of medical history can cause great problems. Therefore, if there is anyone looking for this man who was with H.Q. Army, APO 230, they should know that their medical background is waiting to be revealed.

Heather D. of Maryland is looking for a half-brother who she knows was adopted in 1959. He was born July 16 in the Victoria Nursing Home in Cheltenham. She knows the name on his birth certificate, but the father's name has been left blank. Since the only other information Heather has is that an adoption took place in Bristol, which does not signify necessarily that this was the home area of the parents, he has yet to be found.

Coincidentally, this case is amazingly similar to one where it is the father in Florida who, now with no other children, is trying to reclaim his only son who was born in Britain. Unfortunately, as a young G.I. in the U.K. in the mid-1950s, he did not pay enough attention to the details relayed to him when he was called in by his Commanding Officer who had received a complaint from the girl-friend.

Now, he has little to go on other than he met her in a pub, which while echoing an earlier anecdote, narrows the odds since this pub was in a much smaller town than London. Rushden is near Northampton; the girl was a local but only 17 at the time and therefore legally underage to be drinking. He may not have been aware of this. Now, all he remembers is her last name. This could make it easier to find her, except she is probably now married; the child was given up for adoption and one would not wish to intrude on her new life.

One just hopes that a few other details may strike a chord of remembrance. The name of the official who handled the adoption was Sister Coombs. The Nursing Home was in Kettering and the child may share an AB blood group with his father. While he was born "Robert" this too may have been changed.

After an early and insistent rush of phone calls and letters from the father, they have ceased, which put me personally on a difficult spot. I had asked a family history researcher to help and she did a lot of groundwork at her own expense. This could have gone further if not for the silence from Florida and sadly, someone out there may still be wishing his father would find him.

Rachel James in Ohio has a little more detail on the children that she knows her father, Rempson Miller, left in the Manchester area of England. His unit was actually based in the town of Burton-on-Trent, but Manchester is the larger city with more amenities and where the men went for their recreation and relaxation. This was obviously where Rachel's father established a long-term relationship; she has found one of her father's wartime friends who remembers the woman bringing children to visit their father.

This friend also fathered a child in the same area. After the war, he saved for the fare to send for the mother and child who had been given his name. He was informed that the woman had died, and the child had been placed in a foster home. He has yet to find him.

Since starting to conduct this search for her British siblings, Rachel has found another of her father's Army friends, on a similar trail. This is only useful information to TRACE if someone has either of the above men on any of their paperwork or the match is made by our membership secretary's phenomenal memory. In this case, the name is common in the U.K. and would not stand out on any adoption paperwork unless the father was also identified as a black G.I.

Unfortunately, we have a greater problem finding black fathers because they do not seem to keep in touch with their old Army units, which is a useful starting point of reference. The National Association for Black Veterans is our second resource but can only help if the G.I. has joined them. In spite of these difficulties, we have had several successes, including one father in Alabama who carried a photograph of his British baby for forty years. When he was found, neither could afford the cost of transatlantic flight until a British newspaper stepped in to reunite them.

Not all the American-based inquiries come in letter form. Two G.I.s visiting England on a mission to find their children had been advised by the American Red Cross in Baltimore that TRACE might help. As they came down my residential road, they may have wondered where the business section began since people assume that we operate from an office. Nor do I suspect that these men anticipated enjoying English tea and cake before a quick tour of Hampton Court, let alone ending up being photographed and written about in the *New York Times*, all of which happened.

As described in the *New York Times* on May 20, 1992, Walter Comer from Pennsylvania had been stationed in an all-black engineering battalion in Cornwall where preparations were being made for the invasion of France; he knew he left behind a daughter. A newspaper story brought forth one candidate, but the facts were not a close enough match. Rachel James, mentioned above, saw this as a new challenge, and using all her skills of research (details of which have yet to be explained to me), managed to locate Walter Comer's daughter, Beverly, who has not been living in Cornwall for some time.

I have since been in communication with Beverly and she has filled me in on her life, which has not been easy. Her mother gave her over to her grandparents to be raised. After the war, the Cornwall village in which she grew up had returned to its isolation and provincialism; therefore Beverly suffered the double stigma of illegitimacy and racism.

However, she rose above it, married, and now lives in another part of England. She has become a well-educated, self-possessed woman. Naturally, her first question to me was "What is my father like?" This put me for the first time in the unique position of having met the father before the child. Having spent a delightful afternoon in his company, all my impressions were favorable. Thanks to Rachel, father and daughter enjoyed a reunion in Philadelphia.

Chapter Twelve

᛭ ᚩᚳᛈ ᚩᛂ

Still Looking

In spite of successes that by now exceed 600, there are still a large a number of people out there searching. In order not to make this a chapter full of woe, only short snippets of stories are included in the hope that some details will be recognized.

Phone calls and letters still come in on a daily basis asking for advice. There now seems to be a preponderance of people who have been adopted into the family. This allows the secret to be even more deeply hidden because there was less likelihood of questions relating to the lack of family resemblance. In such cases, discovery does not seem to occur until a death in the family leaves someone free to tell the truth.

Late as these inquiries may be in relation to the child's age and that of the G.I. parent, they now have the advantage of the Internet, which speeds up their chances of success even if all they have is a name and no location. Although they may search through hundreds of names on a list, it does not stop those who wish to succeed.

The illustrations that follow are representative of these late arrivals. Identities are limited to first names and places that may provide some readers with clues that match up to some of the letters that I receive from conscience-stricken fathers in the States.

Trevor L. in western Australia did not have such a secure home life even though he was adopted by his mother's sister when he was 2 years old. He was told that his real father was a seaman working on the tugboats and that his natural mother had been paid a sum of one hundred pounds compensation by the U.S. authorities. We are aware that this often did happen. It was considered a large amount of money in the 1940s but could not have done much for this man's self-esteem to learn about it.

His foundations were shaken even more when within eleven years both of his adoptive parents died and he was raised by grandparents. When the truth came out, he had to write to his biological mother in England for some background details to try to build his identity. She offered only the father's name and refused to answer any more questions. The problem here is that there could be a variant to the spelling of the last name. Few of the young women who went out with G.I.s at that time had reason to see their name in print.

Trevor does know that his father was in the U.S. Air Force based at Mildenhall or Holton and that his mother was in the Land Army (a group of British women conscripted into work on the land, which was considered as important as putting them in the other services). Trevor says that he will never give up hope of finding his father; without him he feels that he has no roots.

When children are told "family secrets" at a young age, they do not necessarily register, even though in the case of Carole T. of Dorset she was also shown a photograph of her father with two friends. By the time she was old enough to show an interest in this, the photograph had disappeared. She suspects that it was destroyed by her stepfather.

When she grew older, Carole began to feel that something was missing in her makeup and, knowing that her father was an American, she wrote to the Embassy for help. TRACE was on the list of suggestions they sent her as to how she should proceed. Since her father was in the U.S. Navy we gave her two places to start: the locator column of the *Navy Times* and the National Personnel Records Center. In addition, we thought that it might be an idea to run an ad in her local paper to see if some of her mother's friends of that era might respond and remember some little extra detail about this American sailor. The only slightly positive response was from someone who had had a child by one of her father's friends; she said that the men were billeted above a place called Carter's Pottery in Poole Harbour. So far, she has not managed to get any further forward than that.

Sharon W. from Leicester knows that her mother married her father but that it did not work out. This could have been because her father was a gambler who was later dishonorably discharged from the Army. She does not see this as a reason to inhibit her search, but, sadly, there is no longer any opportunity to ask further questions; her mother has died. However, she has her father's name, number, and home state but cannot find him in that direction. Her last chance seems to be the National Personnel Records Center in the hope that his files survived the fire.

Uwe M. from Antrifttal, Germany, is also looking for his father in Pennsylvania. He sent a wad of paperwork to us relating to the registration of his birth. It has not proved as helpful as might be hoped. Experience has now shown us that officialdom does not always get the name or place right when it relates to a foreign country. In this case the father's address could be a box number in a small town in Pennsylvania or a residence on one of four possible streets in Philadelphia. This has yet to be established because the addresses are out of date. Uwe does have his father's name and number, which is usually invaluable when approaching a Veterans Administration office, but since the G.I. was in service in Germany 1961–1962 and probably a draftee, it is doubtful he would have earned benefits to put him on record.

Karl S. of Reichersbeuren, Germany, was born a year after the war ended, so he knows that his father was a member of the Army of the occupation. When he discovered this at the age of 10, he was delighted. It is worth noting that the attitude of these German children of the G.I.s was different from that of their elders. They did not see the the United States in the despised role of the conqueror. These young people had now seen American movies and been injected with the glamor and excitement of that distant country.

Karl has his father's home state as well as his name, but because it is quite a common one, the G.I. is proving difficult to locate. So far, Karl has sent out eighty-five letters to the same named people in Tennessee but has had little response. He also knows that his father was a member of the 3rd American Army, XII Corps, probably 26th Division, but their association does not have him on record nor has the VA office in that state been able to help him.

Paul B. of London has the problem of not being sure if he has the correct spelling for his father's name. He is a 1950s baby, also thrown into the confusion of being adopted by his grandmother and assuming as a child that his mother was his sister. It was not until the late 1970s that he began to ask questions about his father and discovered that, after his mother's unsuccessful attempts to reach him via the Veterans Administration office in Kentucky, she had destroyed all his letters and photographs, which might have held some additional or useful clues.

Paul suspects that his father was a married man at the time he met his mother. He appears to have been a sergeant in the U.S. Air Force at a transit camp in the Dorset area. When he heard about the pregnancy, he managed a swift departure, possibly to Germany where there were many American bases.

Paul has followed up on the Kentucky lead and has discovered that the Cabinet for Health Services there has no record of this G.I. having been born, divorced, or dying within the state. This could indicate that Kentucky was not his home but where he had been based prior to his arrival in Europe, a common misunderstanding. In this case one can rule out the alternative of mistaking the name of the state from the way it was pronounced since there is no other that sounds similar enough to be misheard.

Paul is, unhappily, now at a standstill since no records at the NPRC match any variation on his father's name to a serviceman in Europe at that time. For the moment, he can only cling to the one similarity he has with his father. He, too, is a musician.

David C. of West Sussex was content in his adoption and not concerned about his biological background until after he was married. He found an old diary that had a name alongside a date, which he recognized as his birthday, June 29, 1945. From questions to a relative, he was then able to trace his natural mother. She was not pleased to be found because she was by now married with a family. It was only years later, after she was widowed, that she agreed to answer questions.

David was told his natural father's name and that he had been in the 82nd Airborne. He has not received any response from a letter to the Memorial Museum. The G.I.'s name is Germanic in origin and reasonably common in the States, which is making his finding difficult. All one can add to this particular search is the name of the British mother—Mona—in the hope these few clues might be recognizable.

There is no reason not to include the name of the ship in which a very young G.I. father sailed back to the States. He left his Bible with his British sweetheart, whom his mother would not give him permission to marry. Richard P., who now lives in Wiltshire, was a babe in arms carried down to Southampton to watch the troop-laden *Mauritania* sail away.

This is beyond his memory bank, so he accepted the story that his grandmother fed him—that his father had made a quick exit when he learned of the baby's arrival. It was not until he was 50 when someone remarked how much he looked like his father that the truth came out. So far, he has been unable to find him. In this case, while the last name is reasonably common in the United States, the first one makes it unusual—it matches the last name of president Clinton!

Lynn S. of Hampshire was adopted but knows that her natural parents met in London. This makes finding her father even more difficult. He may, like thousands of other G.I.s, been on sightseeing leave there, not attached to one of the many units operating in the area. His name is common enough to have produced a long list, which she is following up. It has so far produced a very helpful person who, while disclaiming fatherhood, has encouraged her to keep going until she finds the missing G.I.

Under these circumstances, there is always the suspicion that this is the father hiding behind the role of friend, but not in this case. What little information Lynn has since obtained from her natural mother is the consistent clue that the name of her father's hometown starts with "Spring." This can apply to so many towns in Texas, let alone the rest of the United States, that Lynn has been warned that she still has a long search ahead.

Someone from Bretton, Germany, sent us the most amazing wad of paperwork with her letter of inquiry. This included all the letters that her father wrote to her mother, from which can be concluded that this was a relationship of some standing not only with his German girlfriend but her whole family.

She was born in July 1946. Her father registered her birth, and his name and address in the United States are on the certificate. Whether he then left Germany with promises to return is less clear, though the copies of the telegrams that arrived after he was back home indicate that he sent some money for the child's support.

This did not last long, and by 1952, her mother went to the chaplain on base for help. On her behalf he wrote to the sergeant's last known address. It was returned marked "unknown." One could have assumed that he had lost interest in his declared responsibilities except for the fact that some months later the mother received a letter from someone, newly arrived in Germany. He had been asked to inquire of her present situation.

Her letter to TRACE in 1997 indicates that nothing resulted from that inquiry. If alive, her father would now be in his mid-80s. It is possible that this cutoff in communication was caused by him being killed. No one would have known to notify his German child.

Alternatively, he did have photographs taken of himself with his daughter, and if he died more recently one can still hope that, as in similar incidences, someone in his family will try to trace her.

Gillian B.-K. from Hertfordshire shares a similar hope. She did not discover her true background until she was 48. In order to keep the peace within the family, she delayed any searching until after her mother died.

The details of her father are sparse, plus his name, while Scot in origin, is quite common in the U.S. She has, therefore, tried to approach the problem from a different angle by seeking out people who might have been stationed on the same base in Hertfordshire where her parents met. This, so far, has brought her little joy, and she is concerned that so much time has now passed that he may by now be dead, but she cannot bring herself to stop searching. She is encouraged by that fact that her suggestion to Martin L. in chapter 4 resulted in his finding his U.S. family.

Jenny G. of Sheffield has had to tread warily because at the time of her conception, her mother's husband was in prison. She was adopted, and it was not until she found her natural mother that she was able to get fuller details about her G.I. father. It was revealed that once he learned of the pregnancy he managed a transfer to another base where he later met and married a British girl.

Through the internet, Jenny discovered two people with her father's name, and it is very likely that they are related. The one that she spoke to identified himself as her father's nephew. He gave her the town where her father was now residing and promised to send the full address. This did not happen, so one might assume this cousin decided against interfering.

With the new information she had, Jenny returned to the Internet to see if it would reveal that address. Nothing came up, which indicates that his telephone number is unlisted. Rather than intrude or make trouble for this originally helpful cousin, we have suggested to Jenny that she approach her father via a letter from the NPRC, which will look less threatening than one with a foreign stamp. Since then Randolph Air Force Base in Texas has agreed to forward her letter to her father. So far there has been no reply. One can only hope that the recipient will eventually show her some compassion. Most important to Jenny is finding out about her identity.

It has already been seen that the motivation to find a G.I. father can come from the children, but there are now many grandchildren taking up the search themselves. They have more chance of a good result. The G.I. may be apprehensive that behind his long-lost European child is an old girlfriend out to get him, let alone an ex-wife, but a grandchild is not threatening.

Someone from Lincoln is a happy example of how intrigued Grandpa can be to meet his foreign grandchildren. He had married Grandma, but after two years in the States she returned to the U.K. and was reluctant forevermore to talk about the reasons why. Whatever the cause, it did not detract from the welcome she received from her Grandpa in Illinois.

A quote in a letter from Munich shows that the writer worries that so much time has passed she may not be this lucky: "he was a soldier with the rank of Sgt. deployed in the Weiden/Oberpfalz in Spring Summer 1945. He was born in Los Angeles. Perhaps he is still alive. He don't know that he has a son and two grand-daughters in Germany."

A granddaughter of a G.I. stationed in Cheltenham has taken up the search. Her British grandparents prevented their daughter from marrying the G.I. and had the baby adopted into the family. On their behalf, one must reiterate that these G.I.s. represented the "unknown." That generation of parents held Victorian values; they needed to know background before they gave consent to a daughter's marriage.

The fact that this daughter was old enough to be called into uniform during the war did not, in this case, appear to remove their emotional or legal control: "My Gran, Gwen was in the Women's Air Force, based at Castle-Bromwich. My American Grandpa in the U.S.A. based nearby. Gwen was artistic and loved to paint, an uncle has said that G.I. was possibly a professional gambler. They wanted to get married but her parents would not sign the papers. We think he was sent back to the U.S. because of this."

In this case, one can understand the parental apprehension, but it does not now detract from Joanne attempting to find her American grandfather.

Coincidentally, two "Tammies" wrote about the same time early in 1998 in the hope of finding their grandfather. One letter I am recording almost in total length because it illustrates the other motivation behind these searches:

My Mum has done so much for me and is such a wonderful mother that finding her father and fulfilling one of her dreams is the one thing I would love to do. I am 18 years old and doing this myself which is why I desperately need your help. . . . my Grandad, originated from Virginia. He came to Luton in the late 40s. Through this time, he fell in love with my Grandma. She fell pregnant and told my Grandad; this caused many problems because of my Grandma's age [she must have been very young]. . . . my Grandad was called away with the Army before my mother was born, however this did not stop him wanting contact. He even wanted them to move to America. He was never allowed to make contact with them again as my Mum was adopted by her grandparents and every letter my Grandad sent was burnt. My mother grew up thinking her Grandma was her mother and her mother was her sister until she was old enough to understand. She never got any information about her father except from an aunt. His name was . . . and his parents owned a tobacco company in Virginia. I would love to find my Grandad, most of all for my mother's sake. She has faced a lot of heartache through her life. I would love to find her father or even some family on his side. . . . thanks for reading this letter.

Obviously it would be unfair to name any names or to suggest a slight exaggeration in the G.I.'s claim to family affluence—rich boys as well as poor boys went to war. One can only hope that with these minimal clues a young lady might be able to give her mother the gift she feels she deserves—a father.

The other Tammie lives in Somerset. She, too, wishes to find her grandfather on behalf of her mother: "he was an American soldier based in Yeovil 43/44 who left to join the D.Day Invasion. His name is . . . born around 1920. She last heard of him in a letter when she was 6 years old. His last address was Staten Island NY. We also know that he had a sister. Please can you help us with any information, my Grandmother's name was Faith Iona Lewis when they met."

The most poignant part of this particular story is the fact that after the war was over, this G.I.'s ship pulled into the port of Southampton on its way back to the United States. He tried but was not allowed to get off the ship.

Tracey W. of Leicester, courtesy of National Personnel Records Center, knows that her grandfather died in Jasper, Texas. His service record also revealed that he retired in July 1969. What she now wants to do is trace her Indian heritage; there is Cherokee blood in the family and, to her knowledge, there are three uncles to find.

A CD-ROM revealed more than 100 people with her family name, and she phoned some of them, but this proved an expensive exercise. She at last reached a relative and is learning her family history.

To conclude this chapter, I appeal to the G.I. who remembers singing "Silent Night" to his British daughter whose memories of him are centered on Christmas. His granddaughter knows that he was a sergeant with the 101st Airborne. Because he was on the clerical side he rarely left the area. This allowed him to establish a stable relationship with a local girl that went on for several years, and there was a child. At the end of his stay in England, he pleaded for Marjorie and the baby, Karalyn, to go back with him. Family pressure against the idea stopped her.

> In 1960, a Warrant Officer who was a close friend of Grandpa, was assigned to England. He was asked while there to persuade Marjorie and our mother to join him. . . . He had not heard anything in all those years and yet he still lived in hope of seeing his daughter again. . . . He [the warrant officer] arrived at the house to find the family there and they had a deep discussion. He explained that Gerry had gone back to Ohio and was desperate for our Grandmother and mother to join him. His feelings for them were still very strong. Marjorie was now married and not interested. Karalyn was torn between a rose and a thistle; the thistle being the family who said that if she even thought of seeing her father again she would be disappointing and disgracing the family.

How such pressure, let alone lack of feeling, could be heaped on the head of a 15 year old is now hard to conceive. What makes this story even more tragic is that the G.I. father had sent money for his daughter to come to visit him in the States, but it was never passed on. The man who tried to act as intermediary was last heard to be retired in Denver, Colorado. The G.I. father/grandfather is still being sought.

One can only repeat the hope that this representation of anxious and unhappy people badly in need of full knowledge of their identity will be acknowledged by some of the readers. Some family members may perhaps by now have either received a wartime confidence from their father or found papers in his effects that indicate there is the possibility of an additional member of their family in Europe.

Now is the time to claim them.

Chapter Thirteen

꾸 ꙮ ꙭ ꙮ

Summing Up

More than half a century has passed since babies were conceived during one of the most horrific periods of war the world has ever known. The parents of those babies were drawn together not only for all the reasons that young people are always drawn together, but in circumstances that made loving especially urgent since they were all under threat of death and faced a parting that they knew would come at any time and might be forever. In many cases, it was.

It is proving very difficult to wind up this book on the children of American G.I.s in Europe. Even as I write, letters and phone calls are still arriving from people searching for their fathers. As time goes on, fewer and fewer of the old G.I.s will be found alive.

Still, the desire to know at least who one's father was is very powerful. Franklin Combs, who was conceived in France, says "there is no day I don't think of my father. I would have loved so much to give him this love that I have always kept in me for him in case I find him." The questionnaire that went out to people prior to the preparation of this book asked what their reaction would be if they found out that their father was dead. Trevor L., whose story was told in Chapter 12, replied, "I would find his grave and sit with him and wail and tell him I loved him very much." Another man wrote, "It is not that I want to get in contact with him. I only want to know who he was and who I am."

Because of the facts of biology, the identification of one's father is always less of a certainty than identification of one's mother. Wars have severed men from their women and children throughout history. For the European children of the G.I.s, being united with their fathers is not merely contingent upon their father's surviving the war and coming home, since home for the G.I. was thousands of miles away from Europe. As we have seen, even in cases where the parents had married, the reality of moving so far from all their loved ones was too daunting for many European women, and it was easier to part from their child's father than it was to leave behind all that was familiar and dear to them.

An absent or unknown father is a nagging ache for a child and when one determines to find that father, the search is an all-consuming task. For people who discover that their father has died, the pain is often mitigated just by having identified him and found out about him, and perhaps by meeting other members of the family.

My hope is that all who undertake this search will meet with a measure of success, and that they will gain a sense of closure and peace. As was mentioned earlier, the records kept for TRACE are very basic. Members' cards are separated into boxes marked "ongoing" and "success." My ambition has always been that the "successes" will eventually require the larger box.

About the Author

PAMELA WINFIELD is president of TRACE (Transatlantic Children's Enterprise), a nonprofit group that helps the children of G.I.s find their fathers. She has published several books in the U.K. on social issues. She also lectures throughout the U.K. and Europe on several subjects, the most popular being "G.I. Brides and G.I. Babies."